BLiSS

Cleanse

Your Two-Week Mind•Body•Spirit Guide
to Greater Health and Happiness

Lindsey Smith and Lorraine Miller

RAVE REVIEWS FOR THE
BLISS CLEANSE

"Lindsey Smith and Lorraine Miller are two health coaches on a mission to take cleansing to the next level by bringing awareness to how thoughts affect how we eat and how we live. The *Bliss Cleanse: Your Mind-Body-Spirit Guide to Greater Health and Happiness* is a unique approach to learning to love your food, your body, your life and the world. It's easy to follow, and inspires readers to make small changes that add up to a lifetime of happiness."

Joshua Rosenthal, Founder and Director of the Institute for Integrative Nutrition

"We all need life coaches, and Lindsey's and Lorraine's book can be that for you by showing you how to love your life and body. With the self-love you will find inspiration, and with it, the desire to care for and love yourself through your behavior and decisions related to your seeking, creating, and consuming healthy spiritual, emotional, and physical nourishment."

Bernie Siegel, MD and author of A Book of Miracles and 365 Prescriptions For The Soul

"In this day and age of toxic diet, lifestyle and environment, everyone could use a good cleanse! Let these two ladies guide you toward recovering your health, happiness and bliss, easily and deliciously."

Andrea Beaman, Speaker, HHC, Chef, www.andreabeaman.com

The *Bliss Cleanse: Your Mind-Body-Spirit Guide to Greater Health and Happiness* inspires you before you read a single word. This book is not only beautiful but it's powerful, clean design leads you on a journey to success. Lorraine Miller and Lindsey Smith motivate us to believe we are capable of making changes that enable us to thrive. You feel supported and encouraged every step of the way to your very own Bliss.

MaryAnn Jones, Founder and Owner, Thrive Naturally, www.thrivenaturally.com

Bliss Cleanse is a wonderful opportunity to love your body, biochemically and emotionally, from the inside out. Clinically speaking, as you cool your liver through a cellular cleanse, you cool all emotions associated with the liver; anger, resentment, and emotional repression all give way to love, acceptance, and peaceful expression. As you expand this space of self-love, it will innately spread to the world around you.

Dr. Kathleen Hartford, CEO Health Pyramid Productions, Author, Lecturer and Licensed Integrated Wellness Practitioner, www.drkathleenhartford.com

"In this day and age where we are inundated with 'lose weight quick' schemes, Lindsey and Lorraine have created a down-to-earth, accessible, and straightforward guide to health that honors the interconnectedness of body, mind and spirit. The *Bliss Cleanse: Your Mind-Body-Spirit Guide to Greater Health and Happiness* is your road map for a year of optimal health, happiness and self-love. If you want to change your relationship with your body from the inside out, this is a must-have for your library."

Laurie Erdman, Inspirational Speaker, Coach, Writer and Founder of Chronic Wellness Coaching, www.chronicwellnesscoaching.com

There is no better program out there than the *Bliss Cleanse* to help you Reset and Reconnect to all that is you! Just flipping through these beautiful, insightful pages serves up a dishful of inspiration and a step-by-step process that will help you declutter your body, mind, and spirit. Let Lindsey and Lorraine be your amazing guides on this journey that will infuse you with energy and clear the way for receiving the health and happiness that are meant to be yours. Now, that is true Bliss!

Marilena Minucci, MS, CHC, BCC, Creator, Quantum Coaching Method™ www.quantumcoachingmethod.com

The *Bliss Cleanse: Your Mind-Body-Spirit Guide to Greater Health and Happiness* encompasses all aspects of living – mind, body and spirit – in an inspirational, easy flowing way that will take you through all four seasons with something for everyone. This approach facilitates small life changes, rather than just diet changes, to strengthen the connection between mind, body and spirit for optimal health and bliss. Way to go Lorraine Miller and Lindsey Smith!

Lisa Wolfson, Program Director, You Can Thrive! Foundation, www.youcanthrive.org

This book was written and published in partnership with inCredible Messages Press.

www.inCredibleMessages.com

bliss

(v); Total state of happiness, utter joy

cleanse

(v); A time for renewal; out with the old and in with the new

To contact the publisher, inCredible Messages Press, visit **www.InCredibleMessages.com**

To contact the authors, visit **www.BlissCleanse.com**

Printed in the United States of America.

978-0-9889266-0-8   Paperback
978-0-9889266-1-5   e-Book
BODY, MIND & SPIRIT / Inspiration & Personal Growth

Photos pages 52, 67, 116, 162, and 206 by Dana Scheller of Scheller Image and Company.

Photo page 68 by Lorraine Miller.

All other photos by: Rosie Fodera, www.fotocouture.com

Styling by Mimma Fico, www.sweetfreedomblog.blogspot.com

Design, layout and illustration by Lorraine Miller Design, www.lorrainemillerdesign.com

To all of our Bliss Cleansers,

May you find purpose,

passion, joy, and success

on your journey to bliss.

dedication

"When you realize there is nothing lacking,
the whole world belongs to you."

–From Tao Te Ching
by Lao Tzu

gratitude

Our sincere gratitude to **Joshua Rosenthal,** Founder and Director of the
Institute for Integrative Nutrition, for guiding us to finding our own bliss and
inspiring us to help make the world a healthier, happier place.

Many thanks to our editor, **Ashley Boynes-Shuck**
for your tireless work and determination.

Special thanks to our photographer, **Rosie Fodera,** and our stylist,
Mimma Fico, for your creative genius. The bliss photos are beyond beautiful!

To **Dana Scheller,** thank you for your gorgeous food photos—delicious!

Thank you to **Jon Andreyo** and **Roger Kean,** our video experts,
for your talent and generosity.

Thank you to **Jamey Stewart** of Mega Media Factory for your
countless effort in making our website run smoothly.

Thank you to **Aimee Woods** of Embody Natural Health
for lending your beautiful space to shoot our video.

To our superheroes, **Daniel** and **Derek,** for your amazing love and support!

congratulations!

Congratulations on embarking on this
two-week journey with us!

We are so excited you have made the choice to get started on your path to

vibrant health and lasting happiness by participating in this one-of-a-kind cleanse.

We wish you amazing success as you nourish mind, body, and spirit, a true

expression of self-love and self-gratitude. Ready to begin? Let's go!

Love,

Lindsey & Lorraine

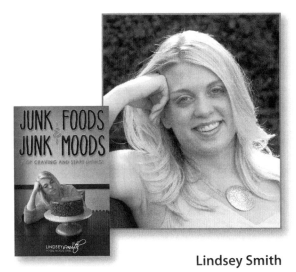

Lindsey Smith
Inspirational Speaker,
Holistic Health and Lifestyle Coach,
and Author of *Junk Foods and Junk Moods.*
www.foodmoodgirl.com

Lorraine Miller
Holistic Lifestyle Coach, Inspirational
Speaker and Author of *From Gratitude to
Bliss®: A Journey in Health and Happiness.*
www.nourishbynature.com

contents

passion

Why we created the BLiSS Cleanse

LINDSEY'S STORY

This journey of nutrition and health I've been on for quite some time has been just that: a journey.

It wasn't long ago when every thought in my brain was consumed with food. Whether it was eating healthy, not eating, or craving junk food, I think I have encountered food in all the ways possible.

It also wasn't long ago when "light" versions of microwavable meals were my idea of healthy, and the only vegetable I liked was broccoli. (I know what you're thinking, who likes broccoli out of everything?!)

The thought of diets, detoxes, and cleanses was exhausting. It was a lot of work, a lot of money, and at the end of the day, I still felt deprived.

I have had many mentors, teachers, and friends along the way who have taught me different theories about nutrition, healthy living, spirituality, self-love, and living my true bliss.

Through these encounters, I started changing areas of my life one at a time. I swapped the microwavable meals for frozen veggies and whole grains until I eventually stopped using a microwave all together.

I went from self-loathing to feeling grateful for simply waking up, until eventually I encompassed my passion and learned how to love myself.

You see; health is a journey, not a destination. We don't one day start an awesome program or diet and suddenly our life's problems are solved. It doesn't matter how much kale or spinach you eat, it won't change the fact that you don't love yourself. And vice versa.

We have bad days, things happen to us, and sometimes we just want chocolate. And guess what? That's okay. It's a part of life. It's a part of nature. It's a part of being human.

To me, the *Bliss Cleanse* is more than just a program; it's a constant step on your health journey. It's a companion you have by your side. It's something you can come back to each day or each season to find a nugget that you can incorporate into your life. It's not a strict diet, but rather a guideline to healthy living. It helps pave the path in the journey you have already begun.

And above all, perfection is not the key. The key is finding your own bliss.

I hope you join us on your journey to bliss!

Xo,

Lindsey

LORRAINE'S STORY

For me, cleansing is one of the highest forms of self-love.

The first time I did a cleanse I was blown away by how much I learned about nutrition and about my body, in particular. For years, I had explored many different diet plans in an effort to feel good on a consistent basis, and had considered myself an above-average healthy eater. But it wasn't until I did a cleanse that I took my physical health to a new level.

In my twenties and thirties I suffered from mild depression, emotional highs and lows, and occasional acne. After years of experimenting with food, emotions, and their relationship to each other, I began seeing health from a holistic per-spective. If we only focus on one area of health—food for example—we are not seeing the "whole" picture. To be truly healthy, we need to view nutrition from a mind-body-spirit approach and find ways to nourish these three areas.

After receiving my certification as a Holistic Health Coach through the Institute for Integrative Nutrition, I wanted to create a program that gave you the opportunity to get to know your body in a new way, yet allowed you to connect with your true being.

In 2011, I met my incredible friend and business partner, Lindsey Smith, author of *Junk Foods and Junk Moods,* and the two of us instantly connected.

Our approach to health coaching is very similar and utilizes many of the same tools we have found to be effective on our individual journeys from struggle to success.

We decided to combine our success tools in one program, and voilá, the *Bliss Cleanse* was born!

It is my hope that this program becomes not only an incredible two-week experience for you, but a stepping stone to your lifelong journey in self-love.

We have intentionally included our favorite tools and inspriational tips to guide you in a way that is doable and fun, and can be practiced up to four times a year. I say, "practice" because this program is not something to do once and move on from. It is designed to do again and again, each time adding that one special gem that keeps you ever-growing, ever-learning, ever-succeeding!

I'm so grateful to be able to inspire you with this program and am sure it will bring you peace and joy on your journey to bliss!

To your health and happiness!

Love,

Lorraine

Bliss means different things to different people. Here are some of our favorite bliss descriptions...

bliss is...

Feeling joyful for no particular reason.

Waking up and my body feels rested.

Being around people who lift me up.

Loving where I live.

Being of service.

Feeling safe.

Stepping out of my comfort zone.

Knowing the universe has my back.

Having people in my life I can count on.

Feeling connected to something I care about.

Feeling grateful.

Feeding my body with foods that make me feel amazing.

Wearing clothes that inspire me.

Relaxing in the middle of the week.

Laughing with children.

Loving my body.

Being fearless.

Enjoying every day.

What does BLISS mean to YOU?

My bliss ...

_____

_____

_____

_____

_____

_____

_____

_____

_____

_____

bliss

WELCOME TO BLISS

Welcome to the start of this incredible journey! Not only is this the beginning of a two-week program that will help you cleanse mind, body, and spirit, it is also a stepping stone for you to enter your next phase on your path to bliss. Whether you are just beginning to explore healthier food and lifestyle choices, or you're simply looking for new inspiration and a more holistic approach, this cleanse is a perfect guide to achieving your health and happiness goals, and creating your life of bliss.

Wherever you are in your life, living a healthy lifestyle is an ongoing process and there is always room for more growth and added success!

One thing we'd like to stress to you as you begin this program: Living a healthy lifestyle is *easy*.

Yes, it's true. We know many people, and you probably do too, who live a healthy lifestyle with relative ease and, as a result, enjoy the many benefits it brings them: vibrant energy, happy moods, physical stamina, mental clarity, and more. Did they get to this place overnight? Absolutely not! What most successful people have done to get to the place of sustaining vibrant health and happiness, is make a series of small changes over a given period of time.

From where you are standing now, whatever your goals may be, you may feel overwhelmed with thoughts of how challenging it's going to be to achieve your goals. But, please be assured, by making small changes, one by one, change becomes easy and transformation happens almost miraculously!

WHO THIS CLEANSE IS FOR

This cleanse is a gentle, whole food-based program and is recommended for anyone who is in good general health and ready to take the next step towards achieving vibrant wellness and lasting happiness. Please have an open mind when beginning this program and be gentle with yourself. Achieving vibrant health is a journey, not a race!

This cleanse is not recommended for women who are pregnant or nursing, anyone experiencing a chronic health condition, or anyone with a compromised immune system without first getting approval from your doctor. If you have any doubts regarding your ability to participate in this cleanse, please check with your doctor.

NOTE: If you are under a doctor's care for any disease, injury or other medial condition, or if you are pregnant or breast feeding, you should discuss your desire to participate in this cleanse with your doctor prior to beginning this program. Participating in this cleanse program is not a substitute for medical treatment. Consult your doctor before discontinuing any treatment or therapy he or she may have prescribed.

WHAT YOU CAN EXPECT DURING THIS CLEANSE

During this program you may experience a variety of symptoms or none at all. Your body's level of toxicity and its ability to release will determine how much you are able detox. Sometimes we are ready to let go, and sometimes we need to be patient.

Because this is a **mind-body-spirit detox,** the program includes exercises and inspiration to help prepare you for emotional release as well as the physical release aided by eating whole and purifying foods. Sometimes unreleased emotions and stress get stored in our bodies as toxins and can keep us feeling stuck. Many holistic practitioners believe, "Our issues are in our tissues."

When we are ready to let go of toxins, including past emotions and negative thought patterns, our bodies may respond by experiencing physical symptoms. These can include skin rashes, sweating, upset stomach, emotional upset, headaches, fatigue or even a fever. These symptoms are sometimes referred to as a "healing crisis" and should be mild and last no more than 1-3 days. As your body releases toxins, you may also find that your clothes are fitting better! Since toxins are stored in our fat cells, detoxing can allow you to shed excess weight.

Whether or not you experience physical or emotional symptoms, trust that your body is doing what it needs to on it's own time. Listen to your body and give it what it asks for. If you're tired, get some extra sleep. If you're hungry, eat something healthy and satisfying. Your body is always communicating with you so get ready to listen.

HOW TO GET THE MOST
OUT OF THIS PROGRAM

While we will be providing you with a wealth of information, tips and inspiration, please keep in mind that we do not expect you to follow through on every recommendation. In fact, we highly discourage it! Perfectionism is not the goal of this program. Letting go of what isn't serving you in order to make room for new growth is the goal. Sometimes that means letting go of perfectionism. What we do recommend is that you read the materials and decide for yourself which parts resonate with you.

Everyone is in a different place on his or her journey. Assess where you are and where you want to go, and then pick a few areas to focus on during these two weeks that you feel will add the most to your health and happiness.

Choose a few personal goals around food such as:

• eliminate refined sugar and caffeine from my diet

• add more greens

• reduce animal products

Choose a few personal goals around thinking such as:

• let go of a limiting belief around weight loss

• practice gratitude every day

• notice how my thoughts affect me physically in my body

Avoid Perfectionism. Remember this program is meant to be something you do again and again. Each time you will find something new to add to your daily routine. It's not about doing everything right the first time. Be patient with yourself.

Choose a few personal goals around spirit:

• find a way to do more (dancing, pottery, traveling) – something I love

• clear away clutter in my office

• love myself more

Whatever your goals are, make sure they are yours. Make them personal. Only you know what you need right now to move forward in the direction of your bliss!

Be patient. As we've said, change doesn't happen overnight. Many of the tools you will learn during these two weeks you will take with you after the program to practice and practice again.

The important thing is that you gain a good understanding of where you are and where you want to go.

Do your best during these two weeks to complete the program with the intention of experiencing what it's like to make better choices to nourish your mind, body and spirit so that you can continue practicing those choices after the program.

start

GETTING **STARTED**

To get ready for this cleanse, there are a few steps to follow:

1. **Clear off your schedule!** We recommend you limit your normal activities during the next two weeks so you can have some extra time to focus on what's really important: your health and happiness. Identify any obstacles that may stand in your way of participating in this program and decide to clear them away during the two weeks you commit to cleansing. If there's an activity that you don't need to do, skip it. You'll want to use that time for food shopping, trying new recipes, practicing self-care and other recommendations you choose to follow. You'll also want to indulge yourself in at least 8-9 hours of sleep per night while you are cleansing.

2. **Set your intentions**
   Before beginning any program, we recommend taking time to set your intentions. The more clear you are about what you want to achieve, and why you want to achieve it, the better your chance for success.

*What are you hoping to achieve
from this program?*

*What will be the benefit to
you once you have achieved it?*

What are ready to let go of?

Make time in your schedule to shop! It's a good idea to set aside some extra time to browse through the health food section of your supermarket or visit a health food store if reading labels is new for you.

Perhaps you are ready to let go of a physical condition such as excess weight, tension, chronic headaches, skin problems, fatigue, or brittle hair and nails. Think about which things you are most ready to let go of.

Next, think about what mental or emotional conditions you want to release such as anxiety, emotional ups and downs, negativity, anger, frustration, or fear. Once you've given that some thought, jot down a few things you are ready to bring into your life, to replace what you will be letting go.

3. **Review the following materials in detail:**
    - *Bliss Cleanse* Guidelines for Mind, Body and Spirit (See pages 25-41)
    - Bliss Seasonal Eating Guide (See pages 42-51)
    - Pantry Must-Haves (See pages 52-55)
    - Bliss Smoothie Guide (See pages 57-59)
    - Bliss Body Recipes (See pages 61-65)
    - Bliss Seasonal Cleansing Guides (See pages 67-265)

4. **Next, it's time to go shopping!** Select which recipes you may wish to make during the next two weeks and decide when you will shop for ingredients. Be sure to read the guidelines about foods and ingredients to avoid and be sure to read labels when you shop.

5. **Start the Cleanse!** When you're ready to start, simply begin following the suggested meal plan for the current season or create your own using the seasonal recipes provided. Remember to follow the Mind-Body-Spirit Guidelines (pages 25-41) and to use the suggested meal plans and daily checklists for each season to keep you on track! Good luck!

vision

....

BLISS **ACTIVITY**

You might choose to make a mini-Bliss Vision Board by placing images on an 8.5 x 11" piece of paper. Include anything that inspires you; anything that represents vibrant health and lasting happiness. What does your vision of bliss look like? Having a visual that you can look at every day helps solidify your intentions.

"If we could give every individual the right amount of nourishment and exercise, not too little and not too much, we would have found the safest way to health."

–*Hippocrates*

MIND
BODY
SPIRIT

GUIDELINES

MIND

CLEANSING YOUR **MIND**

When we think of cleansing, we don't always think of cleansing our mind. But just like your body, your mind can get cluttered with negative thinking and bogged down with overwhelming details that take us away from living our bliss.

The *Bliss Cleanse* is a one-of-a-kind program that takes a holistic approach that allows you to cleanse mind, body and spirit throughout the year.

1. **Check in with your self-talk.** Ask yourself, "Do I feed myself with thoughts that are nourishing, gentle and non-judgmental, or does my self-talk place limitations on what is possible for me?"

2. **Identify any limiting beliefs** such as "I can't lose weight." Instead, replace them with a positive affirmation such as, "I easily let go of excess fat and toxins."

3. **Examine how you feel about food and money.** Should what you put in your body be cheap and of maximum quantity or do you deserve to eat high quality food that you need less of to thrive?

4. **Practice easy meditation:** Take a 5-15 minute break every day, close your eyes and focus on your breath. Breathe in something you are grateful for. Breathe out any stress you may be feeling in your body. If your mind wanders, simply bring it back to your breath. Check out our *Bliss Meditation Collection* at www.BlissCleanse.com for additional guidance.

5. **Practice self-gratitude.** Silently acknowledge yourself for giving your body healthy, nutritious food at every meal as a true act of self-love.

6. **Turn "have-to's" into "get-to's."** Instead of saying "I have to (go to the gym, cook dinner, eat more greens, etc.)" practice saying, "I get to go to the gym and work out today!" "I'm so lucky I have time to shop for fresh veggies." Language goes a long way.

7. **Take a technology fast on nights and weekends.** Avoid sending texts and emails after 5 p.m. every day and on weekends/days off. Your brain needs time to process the work week.

8. **Reflect on at least one positive accomplishment at the end of every day.** If there were things that didn't get done, you can tackle those tomorrow. Don't let them take away from what you did accomplish today.

BODY

CLEANSING YOUR **BODY**

No matter how much we try to eat a clean diet, exercise, and use natural products without harsh chemicals, our body still absorbs toxins from our environment.

Making an effort to cleanse your body a few times a year helps protect you from unwanted weight gain, fatigue, and disease, and will naturally restore your body's ability to thrive.

Cleansing Your Body With *Food*

1. **Drink one glass of water with the juice of one fresh lemon or lime every morning** to help keep your pH in balance.

2. **Aim to eat as many whole, fresh foods per day as possible.** Choose organic whenever possible. Prioritize the "Dirty Dozen" (see http://www.ewg.org/foodnews/summary/).

3. **Avoid all foods containing artificial ingredients, high fructose corn syrup, hydrogenated oils, preservatives and MSG.** Read labels and make a point not to purchase products containing these ingredients. You can't always control the food you eat in a restaurant, but you can control the foods you eat in your own home.

4. **Drink filtered water as much as possible** throughout the day and at least eight 8 oz. glasses. Listen to your body and if you experience headaches, hunger pains, or fatigue, these can be signs that you need more water. For extra hydration, try unsweetened coconut water.

5. **Avoid caffeinated beverages and alcohol** during this program to reduce the amount of toxins your liver and kidneys need to process. If you drink a caffeinated beverage or alcohol, remember to drink at least one additional glass of water to help balance the effects.

6. **Drink peppermint, chamomile, ginger, or other herbal teas with large meals** as the warmth aids digestion. Organic nettle tea also helps cleanse the blood and support your liver and kidneys.

7. **Avoid iced cold beverages with meals** in cooler months as they can slow down digestion.

8. **Eliminate all soda and diet soda** which affect blood sugar and can cause you to get hungry. Instead, drink seltzer with a small amount of natural fruit juice. Do not drink carbonated beverages with meals because they can create gas and hinder digestion.

9. **Use only natural sweeteners:** raw honey, pure maple syrup, organic agave, or stevia. Avoid all foods including breads and sauces that contain refined sugar. Optional: you may choose to avoid all sugars during this cleanse, including natural sweeteners.

10. **Move towards eating a more plant-based diet** and less meat and dairy. *Optional:* you may wish to avoid all meat and/or dairy products during this cleanse.

11. **Choose cold-water fish** that are high in omega 3's and low in toxins such as wild salmon. (See: http://ewg.org/safefishlist)

12. **Switch to sea salt** which contains natural minerals your body needs to function properly.

13. **Slow down when eating and chew your food thoroughly** to help your body absorb essential nutrients. You'll also get full sooner and won't overeat.

14. **Eat as many greens per day as possible.** They contain essential nutrients and cleanse your body from environmental toxins.

15. **Eat only whole grains such as brown rice and quinoa.** Avoid white rice and white flour.

    Optional: For this cleanse, you may choose to eliminate wheat including whole wheat from your diet. Be sure to check all ingredients for wheat or gluten and look for gluten-free foods.

16. **Always balance carbs and protein,** especially if you have a blood sugar issue. For example, eat an apple with almond butter, raisins with nuts, or carrots and hummus.

17. **Experiment with green smoothies,** a great way to get more greens in your daily diet.

18. **Make sure half of your plate has vegetables on it,** 1/4 grain, and 1/4 protein.

19. **When eating out, request a side salad or side order of broccoli, spinach, or other green.**

20. **Keep a food journal** and examine where and when you experience cravings. These are important clues to determining what your body may need to get back into balance.

Dietary Options for this Cleanse:

If you've chosen to eliminate sugar, wheat, and/or dairy completely from your diet during this program, we recommend that you slowly introduce these foods back into your diet after the program, one by one, every three days, and examine any allergy symptoms you may have. These can include headaches, joint pain, sinus congestion, skin reaction, stomach issues, or other symptoms. This process of elimination will allow you to determine if your body is rejecting these foods, because you will experience a noticeable difference when you re-introduce these foods back into your diet. You can also try eliminating soy, corn, or peanuts – other common allergy forming foods.

Cleansing Your Body *Beyond Food*

1. **Give yourself plenty of good, restful sleep.** Your body performs important functions to help the cleansing process while you sleep so make sure you get plenty of it. We recommend at least 8-9 hours per night during the program. Your body is also doing extra work to rid toxins so you may find that you feel fatigued. Take it easy and make a plan to get to bed no later than 10 p.m. each night. Adequate sleep is also necessary for weight loss. If you have trouble sleeping, rub some lavender essential oil on the bottom of your feet and place some on a wash cloth near your pillow. Take a relaxing bath before bedtime and avoid overstimulation from bright computer screens, loud TV, sugar, or caffeinated beverages. Practicing gratitude before bedtime can also help relax you. Make a point to say, "I will sleep well tonight" to yourself and allow yourself to fully appreciate the wonderful gift of a good night's sleep.

2. **Exercise your way to vibrant health.** Exercise and stretching are essential for detoxification. They help increase circulation and allow the body to release toxins through your pores. Try to get 30-45 minutes of exercise at least three times a week during the program. Hot saunas help too! Listen to your body. If you're feeling sluggish, try taking a walk or doing some gentle yoga instead of more strenuous exercise. Keep your body moving but don't overdo it. Remember to stretch and massage your muscles and organs to stimulate cleansing.

3. **Stay hydrated.** Adequate amounts of water are necessary for optimum cleansing to flush toxins from your body. Be sure to get at least eight 8 oz. glasses of filtered water per day, preferably more, during the program. Clean water is something we are blessed with and is something to be grateful for.

4. **Practice Self-Care.** There are a variety of ways to support your body during this program. Here are some of our favorite Self-Care Bliss Suggestions:

Massage: this helps improve circulation and release toxins. If you like massages, this is also a great way to relax. When the body experiences deep relaxation, it is able to balance and heal on its own.

Mineral Salt Bath: these can help your body sweat and release toxins through your pores. Add a handful of Epsom salt or other mineral salt to a hot bath and soak for no more than 20-30 minutes. Add a few drops of lavender essential oil to your bath and light a candle for a relaxing experience. Drink plenty of water after your bath.

Hot Towel Scrub: this can be done 1-2 times per day for up to 20 minutes. Run a washcloth through hot water and wring out excess water. Scrub one section of the body at a time until the skin becomes slightly pink or feels warm. Add more hot water to the towel as needed and complete all sections. Scrubbing has many benefits including opening pores to release toxins, allowing excess fat, mucus, cellulite, and toxins to actively discharge to the surface, reducing muscle tension, improving circulation, and relieving stress.

5. **Detox personal products:** During this program we recommend that you make an effort to switch to more natural personal care products. Many shampoos, lotions, skin care, and other products contain harmful toxins and should be avoided as much as possible. Choose natural brands. Organic coconut or sesame oil is a healthy choice for nourishing your skin.

BLISS TIP

Make your own natural body products

with our Bliss Body Recipes on pages 61-65!

SPIRIT

CLEANSING YOUR **SPIRIT**

So many times we are so focused on eating right and exercising, that we totally forget how to take care of our spirit – that part of us that knows how to be joyful in the moment and doesn't get bogged down by outside situations beyond our control. When we are too "in our head" we forget to listen to our body and we sometimes ignore what the heart wants.

Here are some guidelines to help you nourish that part of you that knows how to be, how to love, how to enjoy. That part of you that says "yes" to life!

1. **Practice daily gratitude.** Simply write down 3-5 things you are grateful for and focus on how you feel when you think about them. We recommend getting a separate journal or notebook to do this, and practicing gratitude either first thing in the morning or last thing before going to bed. *From Gratitude to Bliss*® is an excellent tool to help you begin your practice and is available at www.BlissCleanse.com.

2. **Practice Self-Love.** Instead of focusing on your faults or weaknesses, take time each day to celebrate something wonderful you did, even if it seems small like holding the door for someone. Take some time during this program to remember all the things about you that you love, the parts of you that make you YOU. Allow these feelings to fill your body and nourish you from head to toe.

3. **Spruce up your surroundings.** Clear away clutter in your home or office to allow for new energy to enter. Decorate your space with green plants and inspiring artwork. Celebrate your space and make it yours by choosing items and colors that lift your spirit and make you feel good.

4. **Spend time with nature as a way to stay present.** When we focus on what have now, such as a beautiful sunset, we stay present. This has a way of keeping us in greater balance with the rhythms of nature and nourishes our spirit.

5. **Do something you love.** Do at least one thing each week that really makes your heart sing, something you would feel truly grateful for. Know that this act of self-love will nourish you like no food can.

6. **Spend time with people who make you feel loved, supported, and appreciated.** Try limiting your time with people who drain your energy or create negativity and toxic thinking.

tune in

BLISS SEASONAL EATING GUIDE

to nature

As the seasons change, your body's needs change with them.

Nature gives us different foods at different times of the year to help our bodies adjust to the changing elements. The following are guidelines for tuning into nature and getting the nutrients your body needs each season.

Note: if you live in an area where the temperature is fairly consistent from season to season, simply focus on the Eating Guide that is most appropriate for your location. For example, if you live in the tropics, you can follow the Summer Eating Guide during each season. Get to know the seasonal produce in your area by visiting your local farmers' market.

THE IMPORTANCE OF
SEASONAL CLEANSING

Why cleanse with each season?

There are many advantages to cleansing with each season. Here are just a few:

1. **Let go of excess fat and toxins.**

   Cleansing with each season gives your body a chance to get rid of excess. Just as cleaning out your closet creates a sense of newness and freedom, so does allowing your body to let go of toxic build-up from stress, chemicals in foods, pollutants in our environment, and excess fat from overeating.

2. **Add a new healthy habit to your everyday routine.**

   Doing the *Bliss Cleanse* four times a year allows you to practice adding one or more healthy choices to your everyday routine each time you do it. Over time, you will find that the choices you practice become a part of your life with relative ease.

3. **Stay connected to nature and nourish your mind, body, and spirit.**

   Seasonal cleansing also teaches you how to stay connected to nature and celebrate the abundant gifts available throughout the year. Learning to eat with the seasons is a journey and taking time out to practice this approach is rejuvenating to the mind, body, and spirit.

HOW TO EAT
WITH THE SEASONS

Winter: Think HEARTY and Sustaining. The start of winter signifies a new year. For many, it is a time for post-holiday detoxing. Warming, heavier foods are needed this time of year but remember to keep your diet on the lighter side for this two-week cleanse period. Your body is in rest mode as the days are shorter. This is great time to explore meditation, go inward and do less.

Spring: Think GREEN and Renewal. The earth is waking up from winter and so is your body. The season of spring represents rebirth, renewal, and rejuvenation!

Summer: Think FRUIT, Light and Cooling. The earth is warm and vibrant and your body will need extra support for hydration and cooling. This will give you added energy to stay active to enjoy the longer days. Summer is a great time to explore a new exercise and be outside as much as possible.

Fall: Think ROOTS and Grounding. Fall is the season of letting go. Trees lose their leaves. Lots of change happens. Root vegetables and squashes are plentiful this time of year to help keep you grounded during this transitional time. This is also a time of reflection and gratitude as you prepare your body for winter.

WINTER FOODS

Winter Fruit:

Apples

Cactus pear

Clementines

Dates

Grapefruit

Kiwifruit

Mandarins

Oranges

Passionfruit

Pear

Pomegranate

Red currants

Tangerines

Winter Veggies

Belgian endive

Brussels sprouts

Cauliflower

Chestnuts

Collard greens

Jicama

Kale

Leeks

Squash

Sweet potatoes

Turnips

SPRING FOODS

Spring Fruit:
Apricots
Cherries
Grapefruit
Honeydew
Limes
Mango
Melon
Oranges
Pineapple
Strawberries

Spring Veggies
Artichokes
Arugula
Asparagus
Belgium endive
Broccoli
Chives
Collard greens
Corn
Fava beans
Fennel
Green beans
Lettuce
Mushrooms
Mustard greens
Peas
Radicchio
Rhubarb
Spinach
Swiss chard
Vidalia onions
Watercress

SUMMER FOODS

Summer Fruit:

Apricots
Asian pear
Black currants
Blackberries
Blueberries
Boysenberries
Cantaloupe
Cherries
Elderberries
Figs
Grapefruit
Grapes
Honeydew
Key limes
Limes
Mulberries
Nectarines
Passion fruit
Peaches
Plums
Raspberries
Strawberries
Watermelon

Summer Veggies

Beets
Bell peppers
Broccoli
Corn
Cucumbers
Edamame
Eggplant
Endive
Garlic
Green beans
Lettuce
Lima beans
Okra
Peas
Radishes
Shallots
Summer squash
Tomatoes
Zucchini

FALL FOODS

Fall Fruit
Apples
Cranberries
Grapes
Guava
Huckleberries
Pear
Pomegranate

Fall Veggies
Arugula
Broccoli
Brussels sprouts
Cauliflower
Daikon radish
Endive
Garlic
Ginger
Kale
Lettuce
Mushrooms
Peppers
Pumpkin
Radicchio
Squash
Sweet potatoes
Swiss chard
Turnips

ALL SEASON FOODS

All-Season Fruit
Apples
Avocados
Bananas
Coconut
Lemons
Papaya

All-Season Veggies
Beet greens
Bell peppers
Bok choy
Cabbage
Carrots
Celery
Leeks
Lettuce
Mushrooms
Onions
Parsnips
Shallots
Turnips

BLISS TIP

Appreciate colors. Look around you—there are so many colors to enjoy. When you eat a meal today, notice the colors and appreciate each one, as every color provides you with different nutrients to keep you healthy and happy!

PANTRY **MUST-HAVES**

This is a must-have list for every pantry. When starting your cleanse, it is a great idea to get these items. It helps you have food on hand that can easily go a long way with many dishes. It is also nice to have food to call upon when needed for various recipes.

Canned Goods

Assorted canned beans: black beans, chickpeas, red beans, northern beans, and pinto beans.

Dry Goods/Grains

Quinoa

Couscous

Barley

Brown rice pasta

Brown rice flower

Almond flour

Quinoa flour

Whole wheat flour

Assorted dried beans such as lentils, black beans, and black eyed peas.

Assorted nuts and seeds such as walnuts, cashews, almonds, sunflower seeds, flaxseed, and sesame seeds.

Spices

Assorted dry spices such as bay leaves, cumin, cilantro, turmeric, cayenne pepper, sea salt, black pepper, oregano, sage, paprika, basil, cinnamon, garlic, thyme, curry, and rosemary.

Nut Butters

Peanut butter, almond butter, cashew butter, tahini, sunflower butter.

Oils

Coconut oil

Extra virgin olive oil

Flaxseed oil

Sesame oil

Sauces

Apple cider vinegar

Balsamic vinegar

Red wine vinegar

Braggs Amino Acids

Hot sauce

Tamari soy sauce

Sweeteners

Raw honey

Maple syrup

Brown rice syrup

Agave nectar

Stevia

Fresh Fruits

Apples

Avocados

Bananas

Coconut

Lemons

Papaya

Vegetables

Greens

Bell peppers

Carrots

Celery

Mushrooms

Onions

Parsnips

Shallots

Turnips

Frozen

Blueberries

Raspberries

Blackberries

Strawberries

Bananas

Pineapple

Kale

Spinach

Peppers

Gluten-free bread

stock up

Superfoods

Raw cacao
Maca powder
Hemp protein powder
Chia seeds
Bee pollen
Spirulina powder

Other

Almond milk
Coconut milk
Coconut water
Rice milk
Hemp milk
Vegetable broth
Nutritional yeast

BLISS TIP

Keep it fresh! Get in the habit of shopping frequently for small amounts of fresh produce. Keep some frozen fruits and veggies on hand for those times when you don't make it to the store, or when fresh items are not available.

BLISS
SMOOTHIE
GUIDE

We LOVE Smoothies! Smoothies are an excellent way to jam-pack nutrients into one meal. They are simple, easy to make, and easy to clean up. One of the best things you can do is drink a smoothie every day while cleansing. You will feel more energized, alert, and ready to go for the day.

While there are many recipes for smoothies, here is a main rule of thumb when creating your own:

1. **50% Greens.** The more greens the better. Greens are an important way to cleanse your blood and provide the phytonutrients your body needs to run at optimum efficiency.

2. **25-50% fruit.** This adds natural sweetness that reduces cravings for refined sugar and provides your body with specific nutrients based on the fruit you choose.

3. **Water or almond/rice milk**

4. **Add protein and fat for a complete meal.** To make a smoothie a complete meal on the go, add healthy fat such as avocado, nut butter or coconut oil and your favorite protein powder.

5. **Nutritional Boost**— this is where you can get creative. Here are our favorite boosts: chia seeds, hemp powder, raw cacao powder, raw cacao nibs, and maca powder, etc.

6. **Ice** (for additional thickness in warmer months)

Blend and enjoy!

Smoothie Nutritional Boosts:

Apple Cider Vinegar

Chia Seeds

Hemp Powder

Raw Cacao Powder

Raw Cacao Nibs

Maca Powder

Spirulina Powder

Coconut Oil

Flaxseed

Goji Berries

BLISS TIP

Invest in an individual serving blender. This is great for making morning, on-the-go smoothies or to keep with you at the office. Enjoy nutritious, delicious smoothies all year long!

nourish

BLISS BODY RECIPES

Cleansing is a great time to explore how wonderful it can be to treat your body to natural alternatives that nourish you from the outside in. We've put together this list of Bliss Body recipes to help enhance your cleansing experience, so go ahead and indulge yourself!

BLISS **BODY**

Bliss Body Scrub

Ingredients:
2 cups organic cane sugar
1 cup coconut oil
8 drops of lavender essential oil

Directions:
1. Add sugar to a bowl.
2. Slowly stir in oil until the mixture is smooth. You may not end up using all of the oil.
3. Add essential oils and mix well.
4. Spoon into a glass jar and enjoy!

Cold & Flu Scrub

Ingredients:
2 cups Epsom salt
1 cup coconut oil
5 drops lemon oil
5 drops eucalyptus oil

Directions:
1. Add salt to a bowl
2. Slowly stir in oil until the mixture is smooth. You may not end up using all of the oil.
3. Add essential oils and mix well.
4. Spoon into a glass jar and enjoy!

Bye Bye Bug Repellent

Ingredients:
3 oz. glass or plastic spray jar
Distilled water
50 drops tea tree or citronella essential oil

Directions:
1. Fill spray jar with water ¾ of the way.
2. Add essential oils.
3. Shake and spray! Reapply every so often as needed.

Cinnamon Toothpaste

Ingredients:
2/3 cup baking soda
4 teaspoons fine sea salt
10 drops of cinnamon essential oil
5 drops of tea tree essential oil
Water (until desired consistency)

Directions:
1. Combine baking soda and sea salt.
2. Mix in essential oils.
3. Add water until desired consistency.
4. Store in glass container/jar with closed lid.

Bliss Inhaler

Ingredients:
1 blank inhaler
5-7 drops of eucalyptus essential oil
5-7 drops ylang ylang essential oil
5-7 drops frankincense essential oil
5-7 drops bergamot essential oil
5-7 drops lavender essential oil

Directions:
1. Drop essential oils on cotton wick of the blank inhaler.
2. Close tightly and breathe in when feeling stressed and want to experience bliss.

Gratitude Pillow Mist

Ingredients:
3 oz. glass or plastic spray jar
Distilled water
30 drops lavender essential oil
20 drops lemon essential oil
1 "drop" of "Vitamin G" for gratitude!

Directions:
1. Fill spray jar with water ¾ of the way.
2. Add essential oils.
3. "Sprinkle" some "Vitamin G"
4. Shake mixture up.
5. Spray five sprays on your pillow before you go to bed. With each spray, think of something you have to be grateful for from that day.

Bliss Mask

Ingredients:
2 tbsp. aloe vera gel. (Aloe plants are great for this!)
½ cucumber, de-seeded and chopped
A few mint leaves

Directions:
1. Mix ingredients together in a food processor.
2. Apply the paste to your face for 20-30 minutes.
3. Rinse with warm water and feel the smooth!

Kick the Craving Inhaler

Ingredients:
1 blank inhaler
5-7 drops ylang ylang essential oil
5-7 drops orange essential oil
5-7 drops bergamot essential oil
5-7 drops lemon essential oil

Directions:
1. Drop essential oils on cotton wick of the blank inhaler.
2. Close tightly and breathe in when you feel a craving come on.

BLISS TIP

When washing your hands or your body, give thanks for having warm, running water. Look at even the little things as huge blessings. This will fill you up more than any food ever could.

cleanse

BLISS SEASONAL CLEANSING GUIDES

Let the cleansing begin! Simply go to your current season and review the materials.

WINTER BLISS

CLEANSING GUIDE

On the following pages you'll find a suggested meal plan, healthy and delicious recipes, a shopping list, a daily checklist, and daily inspirations – everything you need to cleanse during winter months!

WINTER BLISS MEAL PLAN

	DAY 1	DAY 2	DAY 3
Morning Bliss	List 5 things you are grateful for	List 5 things you are grateful for	List 5 things you are grateful for
AM Detox Water	Drink 1 glass of water (or cup of hot water) with fresh squeezed juice of ½ lemon	Drink 1 glass of water (or cup of hot water) with fresh squeezed juice of ½ lemon	Drink 1 glass of water (or cup of hot water) with fresh squeezed juice of ½ lemon
Breakfast	Kiwi-Banana Smoothie	Cold Kicker Smoothie	Carrot Cake Smoothie
AM Snack	A Grapefruit	Almond Butter and Apples	Handful of Walnuts
Lunch	Collard Green Wrap	Sweet Potato Soup	Asian Chopped Salad
Mid-Day Snack	Handful of nuts	Ants on a Log	Greek yogurt with pomegranate seeds
Dinner	Spaghetti Squash with Marinara	Collard Green Tempeh Stir Fry	Kale Soup
Night-time Bliss	What's one positive thing that happened today?	List 3 successes that happened today.	Take a mindful walk after dinner.

DAY 4	DAY 5	DAY 6	DAY 7
List 5 things you are grateful for	List 5 things you are grateful for	List 5 things you are grateful for	List 5 things you are grateful for
Drink 1 glass of water (or cup of hot water) with fresh squeezed juice of ½ lemon	Drink 1 glass of water (or cup of hot water) with fresh squeezed juice of ½ lemon	Drink 1 glass of water (or cup of hot water) with fresh squeezed juice of ½ lemon	Drink 1 glass of water (or cup of hot water) with fresh squeezed juice of ½ lemon
Winter Blues Bar	Nutty Cinnamon Quinoa	Peary Good Smoothie	Nutty Cinnamon Quinoa
Hummus and Carrot Sticks	Pomegranate Juice	Celery and Almond Butter	Rice cake (plain or with nut butter)
Wintery Orzo Salad	Power Salad	Bliss Veggie Wrap	Wild Mushroom Soup
Handful of almonds	Apple slices with almond butter and cinnamon	Popcorn with sea salt and crushed walnuts	1 oz. organic dark chocolate square
Endive Pasta	Cozy Quinoa Casserole	Ultimate Burrito	Spicy Cauliflower Bake
Give yourself a hot towel scrub at night.	Make something handmade and give it to a friend!	Take a lavender bubble bath.	Make some ginger tea for comfort.

WINTER BLISS BREAKFAST

Kiwi-Banana Smoothie

Ingredients:
1 kiwi
1 banana
½ cup coconut milk
Handful of ice

Blend all ingredients and enjoy!

_____

Cold Kicker Smoothie

Ingredients:
1 cup raw kale
1 cup blueberries
1 oz. apple cider vinegar
1 tbsp. raw cacao
½ cup water

Blend all ingredients and enjoy!

Winter Blues Bars

Ingredients:
2 cups pitted dates
2 cups raw cashews
½ cup dried blueberries
¼ cup chia seeds

Directions:
1. In food processor, process cashews until they are well-ground (not creamy).
2. Then add dates and continue processing until mixture becomes one sticky ball.
3. Mix in dried blueberries and chia seeds.
4. Line a baking pan or sheet with wax paper. Add mixture and press dough firm and evenly.
5. Refrigerate for 30-40 minutes.
6. Remove from fridge and cut into bars. Individually wrap them so you have an easy snack or a delicious breakfast!

Nutty Cinnamon Quinoa

Ingredients:
½ cup quinoa, cooked
1 tbsp. almond butter
1 tbsp. cinnamon
Handful of slivered almonds

Directions:
1. Warm quinoa, add cinnamon and mix.
2. Add almond butter on top and let melt.
3. Sprinkle slivered almonds.
4. Enjoy!

Peary Good Smoothie

Ingredients:
½ pear
½ banana
½ cup almond milk
1 tbsp. cinnamon
Handful of ice

Blend all ingredients and enjoy!

Carrot Cake Smoothie

Ingredients:
1-2 carrots
½ cup cooked or soaked oats
1 tbsp. cinnamon
1 tbsp. chia seeds
½ cup unsweetened vanilla almond milk

Blend all ingredients and enjoy!

BLISS TIP

Create your own "super smoothies." Add superfoods to your smoothies such as raw cacao, maca powder, bee pollen, spirulina powder, or hemp seed, for added health benefits. *See pages 57-59 for more info!*

WINTER BLISS LUNCH

Collard Green Wrap

Ingredients:
4 large collard leaves
1 red bell pepper, julienned
1 avocado, sliced
½ cucumber, sliced
1 carrot, julienned
½ cup fresh sprouts

Directions:
1. Make dressing and set aside.
2. Rinse collards and cut off the stem. Lay flat.
3. Spread creamy cashew dressing.
4. Fill collard with peppers, avocado, cucumber, carrots, and sprouts.
5. Wrap collard and enjoy!

Creamy Cashew Dressing

Ingredients:
1 cup raw cashews (soaked for 2-4 hours)
1 tbsp. tahini
2 tbsp. nutritional yeast
½ tsp. garlic minced
Sea salt and pepper, to taste

Directions:
1. Drain cashews and add to food processor. Add tahini, garlic, salt and pepper until cashews are gritty.
2. Add nutritional yeast and continue to process until creamy. (You may need to add a little more tahini to get it just right)

BLISS TIP

Try meal prepping for the week. Commit to preparing meals in advance for the week. Use freezer containers to store. This is a great way to ensure you always have something on-the-go!

Sweet Potato Soup

Ingredients:
2 medium sweet potatoes, peeled
   and diced
4 large carrots, peeled and diced
1 medium onion, chopped
1 clove garlic, minced
1 ½ cups vegetable broth
1 ½ cups water
1 tbsp. fresh ginger
1 tbsp. olive oil

Directions:
1. Heat olive oil in large saucepan. Add
   onion and garlic and cook until soft,
   about 2 to 3 minutes.
2. Add broth, water, sweet potatoes,
   carrots, and ginger. Bring to a boil,
   reduce heat, and simmer until
   vegetables are tender, approximately
   15-20 minutes.
3. Strain vegetables and let cool 5
   minutes. Place them in a high power
   blender or food processor. Purée until
   smooth, adding broth as needed.
4. Pour vegetable purée back into the
   saucepan and stir until well blended
   and smooth. Add salt and pepper
   to taste.
5. Enjoy!

Asian Chopped Salad

Ingredients:
2 cups wild rice, cooked
4 carrots, chopped
1 red pepper, chopped
1 yellow pepper, chopped
1 green pepper, chopped
1 cucumber, chopped
1 cup snap peas

Dressing:
Juice of 1 lemon
3 tbsp. olive oil
8 tbsp. apple cider vinegar
2 tbsp. sesame oil
Sea salt and pepper, to taste

Directions:
1. Prepare rice and place in a large
   bowl. Let cool.
2. Prepare vegetables and set aside.
3. Prepare salad dressing by adding
   ingredients and mixing. Set aside.
5. Once rice is cool, add vegetables
   and mix in dressing. Add salt and
   pepper to taste.
5. Enjoy!

WINTER BLISS LUNCH

Wintery Orzo Salad

Ingredients:
1 package orzo (approximately 2-3 cups)
3 carrots, peeled and diced
3 shallots, diced
2 parsnips, diced
2 turnips, diced
½ head of red cabbage, diced
¼ cup olive oil
2/3 cup balsamic vinegar
1 tbsp. raw honey
Sea salt and pepper, to taste

Directions:
1. Preheat oven to 400 ˚F.
2. Prepare dressing by combining olive oil, balsamic vinegar, honey, and salt and pepper.
3. Place diced vegetables in baking dish and toss with dressing. Roast in oven for approximately 45 minutes. Toss every 10-15 minutes. Vegetables will be tender when finished.
4. Prepare orzo as directed. Strain and rinse in cold water. Shake well to remove all access water.
5. Combine orzo with roasted vegetables and toss. Season with salt and pepper to taste.
6. Enjoy!

Power Salad

Ingredients:
2 cups fresh spinach
¼ cup cooked chickpeas
2 tbsp. dried cranberries
½ cup quinoa, cooked and chilled
Juice of ½ lemon
2 tbsp. olive oil
1 tbsp. apple cider vinegar
Sea salt and pepper, to taste

Directions:
1. Place spinach in large bowl.
2. Arrange chickpeas and quinoa in the middle.
3. Sprinkle cranberries on top.
4. Prepare dressing of olive oil, lemon juice, apple cider vinegar, sea salt, and pepper.
5. Pour on salad, toss, and enjoy!

Bliss Veggie Wrap

Ingredients:
1 gluten-free tortilla
2 tbsp. hummus *(see recipe p256)*
Handful of spinach
Leftover peppers, carrots, cucumbers,
   and mushrooms
1 tbsp. dried cranberries

Directions:
1. Lay tortilla wrap flat. Spread hummus to cover wrap.
2. Add spinach and cover all areas of the tortilla.
3. Add vegetables in the center and sprinkle with cranberries.
4. Get your wrap on!

Wild Mushroom Soup

Ingredients:
1 medium onion, chopped
2 cloves garlic, minced
4 carrots, peeled and diced
3 celery stalks, diced
1 pound fresh, sliced mushrooms
6 cups vegetable broth
¾ cups barley
¼ cup olive oil
Sea salt and pepper, to taste

Directions:
1. Heat olive oil in a large saucepan over medium heat.
2. Add onions and garlic. Cook 2-3 minutes until onions are tender.
3. Add the carrots and celery and cook an additional 5-6 minutes until vegetables are tender.
4. Stir in the mushrooms and continue to cook for 5-6 minutes.
5. Pour in vegetable broth and barley.
6. Bring to a boil and then reduce heat. Cover and simmer until barley is tender. Approximately 45 minutes.
7. Season with salt and pepper.
8. Enjoy!

WINTER BLISS LUNCH

Butternut Squash Soup

Ingredients:
1 butternut squash, peeled and cubed
1 bag of carrots (6-8 carrots), peeled
    and chopped
1 large white onion, chopped
3 stalks of celery, chopped
2 garlic gloves, minced
Olive oil
2 or 3 bay leaves
One 32 oz. container of vegetable broth
Sea salt and pepper, to taste
Cinnamon, to taste
Rosemary, to taste

Directions:
1. Preheat oven to 400 °F.
2. Sauté carrots, onion, celery, and garlic
   in olive oil in a soup pot.
   Add salt and pepper to taste.
3. When vegetables are brown, add bay
   leaves and vegetable broth and bring
   to a boil. Once the pot it boiling, bring
   it down to a simmer.
4. Peel the butternut squash, cut in half,
   and scoop out seeds. Discard the
   seeds and cut the squash into cubes.
5. Put the squash on a baking pan and
   add olive oil, salt, pepper, cinnamon,
   and rosemary to your taste. Bake
   25-30 minutes or until tender.
6. Once the squash is done baking, let
   cool. Add squash to blender or food
   processor and purée. Once the squash
   is creamy, set to the side.
7. Take the bay leaves out of the
   veggie broth.
8. With a slotted spoon, add veggies to
   the blender or food processor and
   purée until smooth.
9. Finally, add the squash and vegetables
   back to the vegetable broth. Taste and
   season if needed. Enjoy!

WINTER BLISS DINNER

Spaghetti Squash with Marinara

Ingredients:
1 spaghetti squash
½ cup marinara sauce
Olive oil
Sea salt and pepper, to taste

Parmesan "Cheese"
½ cup crushed walnuts
¼ cup nutritional yeast
½ tbsp. Himalayan sea salt

Directions:
1. Preheat oven to 375 °F.
2. Slice squash in half lengthwise. Using a large spoon, scoop out seeds and discard.
3. Coat large baking pan with olive oil.
4. Place each half of squash down on pan with skin side facing up. Bake for 45 minutes. Flip to other side and bake an additional 15 minutes.
5. Remove from oven. Cool for 5 minutes.
6. Using a fork, scrape out strings of squash and place in large bowl.
7. Heat up marinara sauce in a small saucepan.
8. In a food processor, combine Parmesan "cheese" ingredients.
9. Combine spaghetti squash and marinara sauce. Top with "cheese" and enjoy!

Collard Green Tempeh Stir Fry

Ingredients:
2-3 cups collard greens
1 bunch cauliflower, finely chopped
1 red pepper, chopped
1 small onion, chopped
1 garlic clove, minced
2 carrots, peeled and chopped
1 package tempeh, cubed
1-2 tbsp. sesame oil
Olive oil
Water
Pinch of sea salt and pepper

Directions:
1. Heart large skillet on medium heat and lightly coat with sesame oil.
2. Add garlic and onions. Heat for 3-4 minutes.
3. Add red pepper, carrots, and cauliflower. Heat an additional 5-6 minutes.
4. Cut tempeh into cubes and add to the skillet. Heat an additional 5-6 minutes.
5. Once vegetables and tempeh are browned, add collard greens and cover. You may need to add a little water to help steam.
6. In 4-5 minutes, the collards should be tender. Sprinkle with a pinch of salt and pepper and toss in the pan.
7. Take off heat and enjoy!

WINTER BLISS DINNER

Kale Soup

Ingredients:
8 cups vegetable broth
8 cups kale, de-stemmed, chopped,
  and rinsed
½ large onion, chopped
2 garlic cloves, minced
5 large carrots, peeled and chopped
1 large sweet potato, peeled and cubed
½ cup dry lentils
Olive oil
Sea salt and pepper, to taste

Directions:
1. In a large saucepan, cook the onions and garlic in the olive oil on medium/high heat for about 5-7 minutes. Cover the pan and cook until brown around the edges.
2. Remove the lid, add carrots, salt, and pepper, and cook another 5-7 minutes.
3. Then add vegetable broth, sweet potatoes, and lentils.
4. Allow the soup to come to a full boil and then turn the temperature to low and continue to cook for 25-30 minutes.
5. Add kale and cook 5-10 minutes before serving. Allow kale to wilt in the soup mixture.
6. Take the soup off the heat and enjoy!

Endive Pasta

Ingredients:
1 lb. brown rice pasta, cooked
1 head endive, rinsed and chopped
2 garlic cloves, minced
3 shallots, chopped
¼ cup toasted pine nuts
½ cup raisins
2 tbsp. olive oil

Directions:
1. Boil water and add brown rice pasta. Once pasta is cooked, set aside.
2. In large skillet, heat olive oil on medium heat. When hot, add the garlic and shallots. Cook until shallots are a light brown.
3. Add the chopped endive and raisins and sauté for 2-3 minutes.
4. Combine the pasta and vegetable mixture and toss.
5. Serve with sprinkled pine nuts and enjoy!

Cozy Quinoa Casserole

Ingredients:
1 ½ cups dry quinoa
3 cups vegetable broth
One 15 oz. can black beans, drained
1 large sweet potato, peeled and cubed
1 red pepper, diced large
½ red onion, chopped
2 tbsp. olive oil
1 tbsp. cumin
Salt and pepper, to taste

Directions:
1. Preheat oven to 450 °F.
2. Prepare quinoa as directed. Use the vegetable broth instead of water.
3. Once sweet potatoes, peppers, and onions are prepared, toss them in a bowl with olive oil and salt and pepper.
4. Add vegetable mixture into a casserole dish and bake for 25 minutes or until sweet potatoes are tender.
5. Once the quinoa is cooked, remove from heat and add the black beans and cumin. Set to the side and cover.
6. Once the vegetables are tender, remove from oven. Add quinoa to the casserole dish with the vegetables.
7. Mix and enjoy!

Ultimate Leftover Burrito

Ingredients:
1 gluten-free tortilla
Leftover quinoa casserole
Dollop of fresh salsa
Additional toppings of choice

Directions:
1. Heat up leftover quinoa casserole.
2. Heat up tortilla shell.
3. Add quinoa and toppings and fold like a burrito.
4. Enjoy!

WINTER BLISS DINNER

Spicy Cauliflower Bake

Ingredients:
6 cups cauliflower florets
3 chopped plum tomatoes
2 cloves garlic, minced
Juice of ½ lemon
¼ cup olive oil
½ tsp. turmeric
A pinch of cayenne pepper
Sea salt and pepper, to taste

Directions:
1. Preheat oven to 450 °F.
2. Combine cauliflower and tomatoes in baking pan. Toss with olive oil, lemon juice, garlic, and spices.
3. Bake approximately 25 minutes or until cauliflower is tender.
4. Serve with a side of left over quinoa or rice.

BONUS

For additional snack, drink, and dessert recipes for all seasons, see pages 255-265!

give thanks

Say a prayer or moment of thanks before every meal.
Appreciate how it nourishes your body. Regardless of
what the meal is, give thanks. Your digestive tract will
love you for it!

WINTER BLISS SHOPPING LIST

Vegetables

Kale
Carrots
Collard greens
Cucumber
Assorted peppers: green, yellow, and red
Sprouts
Sweet potatoes
Onions
Garlic
Ginger
Sugar snap peas
Shallots
Parsnips
Red cabbage
Turnips
Spinach
Mushrooms
Celery
Butternut squash
Spaghetti squash
Cauliflower
Endive
Plum tomatoes

Fruits

Lemons
Kiwi
Bananas
Blueberries
Pitted dates
Pears
Avocados

Herbs

Parsley

Grains

Oatmeal
Rolled oats
Quinoa
Wild Rice
Orzo
Barley
Tempeh
Brown rice pasta

Other

Raw cacao
Cashews
Chia seeds
Nut butters
Nutritional yeast
Vegetable broth
Chickpeas
Dried cranberries (unsweetened)
Gluten-free tortilla
Marinara sauce
Walnuts
Lentils
Pine nuts
Raisins
Black beans
Salsa

BLISS TIP

For your convenience, this list is available to download and print at **www.BlissCleanse.com/wintershoplist**

The Daily Bliss Checklist is a wonderful tool to help you stay on track each day of the two-week program. For your convenience, this list is available to download and print at www.BlissCleanse.com/checklist

focus

DAILY **BLISS CHECKLIST**

Today's Date:_____

- ❑ Start my day with a positive thought such as: "Today is a great day!"
- ❑ Balance my body by drinking 16 oz filtered water with fresh squeezed juice of ½ lemon upon waking.
- ❑ Say my favorite affirmation(s) in front of the mirror in the morning. (Examples: "I love my body," "I am beautiful," "I live my bliss," "I am healthy, vibrant, and whole.")
- ❑ Reflect on 3-5 things I am grateful for, jotting them down in my gratitude journal, and notice how I feel when I think about them, either at morning or night.
- ❑ Choose a self-care activity for today and a time I will do it:
  - ❑ detox bath/time:_____ ❑ hot towel scrub /time: _____
  - ❑ listen to the guided meditations/time:_____   other/time:_____
- ❑ My exercise plan for the day and time I will do this:
  - ❑ walk or run/time:_____ ❑ workout at the gym/time:_____
  - ❑ yoga/exercise class/time: _____ ❑ other/time: _____ ❑ rest day
- ❑ If I'm on the go today, then pack healthy snacks such as raw nuts and seeds, cut carrots and celery, and fresh or dried fruit, along with filtered water, so I'll have them on hand when hunger strikes.
- ❑ Drink at least 64 oz. of filtered water and herbal teas. Drink even more when I can to aid the cleansing process.
- ❑ Review Today's Daily Bliss Inspiration. Try out any recommended activities that inspire me.
- ❑ Eat a healthy and satisfying breakfast, review my *Bliss Cleanse* Guidelines if necessary. Follow my Seasonal Cleansing Guides with recipes and meal plans for ideas.
- ❑ Eat a healthy mid-morning snack.
- ❑ Eat a healthy and satisfying lunch. This should be my biggest meal of the day.
- ❑ Eat a healthy afternoon snack.
- ❑ Eat a light, clean, yet satisfying dinner. Cook enough for at least two meals. My dinner should be 50% or more greens.
- ❑ One thing I appreciate about myself today: _____
- ❑ One thing I am looking forward to tomorrow: _____
- ❑ End my day with a positive thought such as, "I had a wonderful day and now I will have a wonderful rest."
- ❑ Get at least 8-9 hours of sleep.

get inspired

YOUR WINTER BLISS
DAILY INSPIRATIONS

We are so excited to bring you our daily inspirations, the ***prized gem of this program!*** Be sure to allow time each day to read and experience these most powerful tips.

If you feel the tendency to say, "I'll do it later," then commit now to giving yourself permission to complete each day's exercise on the day it was intended, rather than put it off, in order to fully embrace the purpose and intention of your mind-body-spirit *Bliss Cleanse*. You are worth it!!!

By following these tips each day, you will nourish yourself with the self-care needed to truly benefit from this program. Remember it's not about doing every-thing, it's about doing a few things each day to support you on your path to bliss.

What's great about these inspirations is that you have them to use after the cleanse is over!

Celebrate your success on taking this journey. You owe it to yourself!

Love,

Lindsey & Lorraine

DAY **ONE**

Since today is the first day of the Winter *Bliss Cleanse,* we want you to set your intentions *in writing.* Your chances of succeeding with this or any program are greatly increased when you set an intention. This helps you get clear on what you want to achieve.

So grab a journal or notebook or use the space below and let's get started!

What are you hoping to achieve from this program?

What will be the benefit to you once you have achieved it (your "WHY")?

What are ready to let go of? Perhaps you are ready to let go of a physical condition such as excess weight, tension, chronic headaches, skin problems, fatigue, or brittle hair and nails. Think about which things you are most ready to let go of. Next think about what mental or emotional conditions you want to release such as anxiety, emotional ups and downs, negativity, anger, frustration, or fear. *Write them down.*

What are you ready to bring in? Now write down a few things you are ready to bring into your life, to replace what you will be letting go. How do you want to feel come spring?

When you're finished, take a moment to thank yourself for completing today's activity!

DAY **TWO**

Today is all about gratitude!

Simply write down 3-5 things you are grateful for, and focus on how you feel when you think about them. We recommend getting a separate journal or notebook to do this, and practicing gratitude either first thing in the morning, or last thing before going to bed. *From Gratitude to Bliss*® is an excellent tool to help you begin your practice. Plan to practice gratitude every day during this cleanse and beyond.

When you're finished, take a moment to thank yourself for completing today's activity!

DAY **THREE**

We live in such a fast-paced society, that we often forget to slow down and appreciate the moment. We not only forget to slow down and appreciate the moment, but we forget to slow down and appreciate our food.

For today, really appreciate your food for nourishing you and taking care of your body. Take time to slow down and appreciate each bite and chew. Really notice the taste, smell, color, and texture of the food before you. Think about how eating winter foods such as healthy soups and winter squashes helps you stay in tune with the season. Put your fork down after every bite. Breathe, be silent, and give thanks.

Write down any differences you notice. Is this something you can work on incorporating on a daily basis?

When you're finished, take a moment to thank yourself for completing today's activity!

DAY **FOUR**

"What we think about ourselves becomes the truth for us ... Every thought we think is creating our future. Each one of us creates our experiences by our thoughts and our feelings. The thoughts we think and the words we speak create our experiences."

–Louise Hay, *You Can Heal Your Life*[1]

How are you talking to yourself today? Are you lifting yourself up or are you tearing yourself down?

Pay extra attention to how you are talking to yourself. Notice when you say something negative and try to replace it with something positive instead.

For example, if you find yourself saying, "It's just so hard for me to lose weight." Instead say, " I love my body and it's easy to lose weight."

It may sound silly at first, but over time, you will start thinking better and feeling better!

When you're finished, take a moment to thank yourself for completing today's activity!

[1] Hay, Louise. You Can Heal Your Life. New York: Hay House, 1984.

DAY **FIVE**

Are you being present in day-to-day situations?

Start by simply being present in your own life. Find peace and joy in nature and your surroundings. Smile at someone walking down the hall or the sidewalk. Simply put, just be.

Appreciate the current moment for what it is, right now. Make it a discipline to stop and appreciate each moment in your life.

Challenge yourself with this exercise:

Take a mindful walk and...

- Walk slowly.
- Stop.
- Look at the intricate details in your surroundings. What changes have you noticed now that it's winter?
- See the veins on leaves, the insects crawling on trees, and the different colors in front of you.
- Now hear the birds chirping, the wind blowing in the background, or the crinkle of leaves beneath animal feet.
- Stop once again. Would you have noticed these things if you had not made the effort to be present?

When you're finished, take a moment to thank yourself for completing today's activity!

DAY **SIX**

You're almost halfway through the mind-body-spirit *Bliss Cleanse* and you are doing an amazing job! When you give your body time to rest and replenish, you start feeling so much better!

Because we are all bio-individually different, however, we all respond to cleansing differently at first.

Pay attention to how are you feeling this week—emotionally and physically. Are you more energetic and happy? Or are you more lethargic and moody?

Pay attention to how your body is feeling and reacting. Journal your thoughts!

When you're finished, take a moment to thank yourself for completing today's activity!

DAY **SEVEN**

It's one thing to eat healthy and cleanse yourself physically, but it is also just as important to cleanse yourself emotionally.

Often times, we let past wounds take foot in our lives and shape us into someone we are not. So instead of dwelling, we want you to list all the reasons why you are amazing! Shifting from a negative to a positive light can not only spread happiness, but it can also shed "weight" we have been carrying around for years.

Why are YOU amazing? What qualities make you amazing, inside and out?

Embrace those qualities by recording them below. When you aren't feeling so good about yourself, look back on your list and remember all your beautiful qualities.

I am amazing because:

When you're finished, take a moment to thank yourself for completing today's activity!

DAY **EIGHT**

You're halfway there! WOOO-HOOO! Way to go! Stop and appreciate this success and the other successes along the way.

We are always trying to get to an end result, and we often dismiss the small successes along the way. Stop and appreciate the successes you had just this morning: making yourself a delish breakfast, taking the kids to school, or sending out a birthday card.

You have accomplished a week-long cleanse! That is a huge success in itself! What other successes have you noticed this week? Take a moment to reflect on all the good that has happened this past week. Write them down!

My recent successes:

When you're finished, take a moment to thank yourself for completing today's activity!

DAY **NINE**

Take some time and focus on stretching today – whether it is in the morning, at your work desk, at a meeting, etc.

Take some time to do some simple stretches to get your blood flowing!

Stretching not only increases your flexibility and helps relieve pain, but it can also generate better blood circulation which helps brings nutrients to your cells AND flushes out toxins. So really, it's a win-win!

Get stretching!

When you're finished, take a moment to thank yourself for completing today's activity!

DAY **TEN**

It's no secret that regular exercise is good for you. It's not only important to try light exercises that help you stretch and strengthen, but it's also important to try exercises that help you break a sweat! Sweating helps release built-up toxins and also helps tighten your skin!

Not there yet? Listen to your body and take it slow. If you're feeling a little tired, get outside and walk! A 10-minute walk is enough to increase energy and improve mood for up to two hours!

When you're finished, take a moment to thank yourself for completing today's activity!

DAY **ELEVEN**

Focus on spreading your love and light into the world by paying it forward. Focus today on doing small things for others. These small things could make a huge difference in someone's life!

Here are some suggestions to get you started, but remember to use your creativity and make this practice authentic to you! Use the space at the end to add your own ideas. Try something new with each season.

- Buy a stranger coffee when you find yourself waiting line
- Put a quarter in a meter that is about to expire
- Smile at a stranger
- Tip a server generously
- Donate to your favorite charity
- Compliment someone in the checkout line
- Volunteer at a local shelter
- Hold the door for someone
- Offer advice to a friend
- Invite someone to cut in front of you at the grocery store
- Donate blood
- _____

- _____

- _____

- _____

- _____

When you're finished, take a moment to thank yourself for completing today's activity!

DAY **TWELVE**

Take some time out today to focus on meditation. Meditation is a way to let go of outside stressors and key in on what's really important!

Practice Easy Meditation: Take a 5-15 minute break every day, close your eyes and focus on your breath. Breathe in something you are grateful for. Breathe out any stress you may be feeling in your body. If your mind wanders, simply bring it back to your breath.

Also check out the *Bliss Meditation Collection* for a guided approach to getting started, available at **www.BlissCleanse.com/shop.**

When you're finished, take a moment to thank yourself for completing today's activity!

DAY **THIRTEEN**

Cleansing in all areas is really important. We have been working on the body and the mind, but today let's look at your space!

Out with the old; in with the new! "Spring" cleaning can be the most cleansing act of them all and can be done with each season! Whether it's sorting through and clearing out old clothes, organizing your closets and kitchen cabinets, or finishing incomplete projects, cleaning up is a refreshing and feel-good process. Hello, peace of mind!

Start small with one space or room and work your way up! You will be complete before you know it! And remember—it's not a race!

If this seems too overwhelming, simply aim to de-clutter at least one area of your home—a room, a closet, or your files—with each season.

When you're finished, take a moment to thank yourself for completing today's activity!

DAY **FOURTEEN**

Congratulations!

Today is the last day of your *Bliss Winter Cleanse!* Stop and savor your success in taking this amazing journey to your health and happiness. Reflect on the areas you want to continue with and set your intentions moving forward.

Honor those intentions. Move forward blissfully. And remember that small changes lead to big results!

Woo-hoo!
Way to go!!!

take note

BLISS TIP

Use the pages that follow to make notes during the Winter *Bliss Cleanse.* These will prove helpful when you return this spring!

TODAY'S DATE:

What I found helpful...

What I found challenging...

TODAY'S DATE:

· ·

What I want to work on next time...

Recipes I want to try next time...

TODAY'S DATE:

....

TODAY'S DATE:

TODAY'S DATE:

....

TODAY'S DATE:

TODAY'S DATE:

· ·

TODAY'S DATE:

TODAY'S DATE:

· ·

TODAY'S DATE:

· ·

SPRING
BLISS
CLEANSING GUIDE

On the following pages you'll find a suggested meal plan, healthy and delicious recipes, a shopping list, a daily checklist, and daily inspirations – everything you need to cleanse during spring months!

SPRING BLISS MEAL PLAN

	DAY 1	DAY 2	DAY 3
Morning Bliss	List 5 things you are grateful for	List 5 things you are grateful for	List 5 things you are grateful for
AM Detox Water	Drink 1 glass of water (or cup of hot water) with fresh squeezed juice of ½ lemon	Drink 1 glass of water (or cup of hot water) with fresh squeezed juice of ½ lemon	Drink 1 glass of water (or cup of hot water) with fresh squeezed juice of ½ lemon
Breakfast	Bliss Energizer	Fruit and Nut Soaked Oats	Bliss Green Smoothie
AM Snack	Fresh Fruit	Edamame Beans	Handful of Almonds
Lunch	Apple Choy Slaw	Bliss Quinoa Salad	Tomato and Avocado Salad
Mid-Day Snack	Mixed Veggies and Hummus	Handful of Pumpkin Seeds	Handful of Olives
Dinner	Easy fried brown rice	Quick and Yummy Sesame Kale	Baked Stuffed Peppers
Night-time Bliss	What's one positive thing that happened today?	List 3 successes that happened today.	Take a mindful walk after dinner.

DAY 4	DAY 5	DAY 6	DAY 7
List 5 things you are grateful for	List 5 things you are grateful for	List 5 things you are grateful for	List 5 things you are grateful for
Drink 1 glass of water (or cup of hot water) with fresh squeezed juice of ½ lemon	Drink 1 glass of water (or cup of hot water) with fresh squeezed juice of ½ lemon	Drink 1 glass of water (or cup of hot water) with fresh squeezed juice of ½ lemon	Drink 1 glass of water (or cup of hot water) with fresh squeezed juice of ½ lemon
Chocolate Covered Strawberry Shake	Breakfast Quinoa	Oatmeal Pancakes	Bliss Energizer
Veggie Muffin	Celery and Almond Butter	Fresh Fruit	Rice cake (plain or with nut butter)
Basic Quinoa Salad	Mushroom and Collard Greens Stir Fry	Apple Chard Salad	Swiss Chard Salad
Tortilla Chips + Salsa	Coconut Water Rice Pudding	Plain Yogurt with Grapefruit	Plain Popcorn
Go Green with Roasted Green Beans and Shallots	Veggie Stir Fry	Mushroom Steaks	Split Pea Soup
Give yourself a hot towel scrub at night.	Make something handmade and give it to a friend!	Take a lavender bubble bath.	Make some ginger tea for comfort.

SPRING BLISS BREAKFAST

Bliss Green Smoothie

Ingredients:
½ cup of your choice chopped greens
   (spinach, kale, dandelion, or another
   favorite green)
1 banana
½ cup almond or rice milk

Blend ingredients and enjoy!

Bliss Energizer

Ingredients:
1 bunch of kale, finely chopped
2 carrots
1 cucumber
1 lemon

Directions:
1. Juice all ingredients with a juicer.
2. Enjoy!

*Note: add a slice of ginger tor a dash of
cayenne pepper for an added kick!*

Fruit & Nut Soaked Oats

Ingredients:
1 cup rolled oats
¼ cup dried fruit (such as blue-berries,
   raisins, cranberries, currants)
Handful of almonds
Water

Directions:
1. The night before, place all ingredients
   in a bowl or mason jar, then fill about
   ½ inch above oats with water.
2. Cover or seal.
3. Place in a cool, dry place overnight.
4. In the morning, warm with a bit of
   water over the stove or eat at room
   temperature.

Note: This makes for a great on-the-go
breakfast! Mason jars are convenient
and easy. Also try adding seeds or your
favorite toppings!

Breakfast Quinoa

Ingredients:
½ cup quinoa, cooked
1 tbsp. cinnamon
1 tbsp. maple syrup
Handful of almonds

Directions:
1. Cook quinoa as directed
2. Mix ½ cup quinoa with cinnamon,
   maple syrup, and almonds. Enjoy!

Chocolate Covered Strawberry Shake

Ingredients:
6 frozen strawberries
1 banana
1 tbsp. raw cacao
½ cup coconut milk

Blend all ingredients and enjoy!

Oatmeal Pancakes

Ingredients:
1 ½ cup oatmeal
½ cup whole wheat flour
2 teaspoon baking powder
2 teaspoon cinnamon
1 tablespoon nut butter
1 banana, chopped
1 ¼ cup almond or rice milk

Directions:
1. Mix dry ingredients together in a
   medium size mixing bowl.
2. Add almond milk and mix.
3. Add nut butter and banana to mixture.
4. Lightly grease pan with olive or canola
   oil and turn on medium heat.
5. Pour batter into small round pancakes
   and heat until batter is fully cooked or
   when sides are golden brown.
6. Enjoy!

BLISS TIP

Create your own "super smoothies." Add superfoods to your smoothies such as raw cacao, maca powder, bee pollen, spirulina powder, or hemp seed, for added health benefits. *See pages 57-59 for more info!*

SPRING BLISS LUNCH

Apple Choy Slaw

Ingredients:
5 stalks of bok choy, chopped
1 granny smith apple, sliced
½ small red onion, thinly sliced
½ cup alfalfa sprouts (optional)

Dressing:
2 tbsp. apple cider vinegar (or
    lemon juice)
2 tsp. honey or brown rice syrup
1 tsp. ground coriander
1 tsp. Dijon mustard
¼ cup olive oil

Directions:
1. Combine all ingredients in a bowl.
2. Prepare dressing in a bowl or shaker
   container and mix well.
3. Pour dressing over salad.
4. Eat immediately. If you are going
   to serve the salad later on, add the
   apples just before serving to prevent
   them from browning.

Bliss Quinoa Salad
Great for a side or a full salad!

Ingredients:
1 ½ cups quinoa, cooked
3 cups water
¼ cup lime juice
½ cup olive oil
1 cup parsley, chopped
½ cup scallion, chopped
½ cup tomato, diced
Additional chopped vegetables
   of your choice
Salt & pepper to taste

Directions:
1. Rinse quinoa well with cool water in
   a fine mesh strainer until the water
   runs clear.
2. Add rinsed quinoa to sauce pan over
   low heat; stir with wooden spoon until
   all water has evaporated and grains
   emit a faint, roasted aroma.
3. Add water and a pinch of salt; stir
   once to dislodge any grains that may
   be stuck to bottom of pan.
4. Cover and bring to boil.
5. Lower heat and simmer, covered, for
   about 10-15 minutes, or until all water
   is absorbed; let sit, covered, for about
   5 minutes before fluffing with fork.
6. Combine all ingredients in bowl and
   serve room temperature.

Tomato and Avocado Salad

Ingredients:
1 avocado
1 tomato
2 garlic cloves, minced
¼ cup cilantro, chopped
Juice of ½ lemon
1 tbsp. olive oil
½ tbsp. Himalayan sea salt

Directions:
1. Cut and cube avocado and tomato, and place in bowl.
2. Chop cilantro and add.
3. Mix in lemon juice, garlic, olive oil and salt.
4. Lightly toss and enjoy!

Swiss Chard Salad

Salad Ingredients:
3 cups swiss chard, chopped
1 red pepper, chopped
1 green pepper, chopped
1 cucumber, chopped
¼ cup unsweetened dried cherries

Dressing Ingredients:
¼ cup olive oil
2 tbsp. fresh lemon juice
½ tsp. Dijon mustard
1 tsp. fresh thyme, chopped
1 clove garlic, minced
½ tsp. Himalayan sea salt

1. Combine salad ingredients in a large bowl.
2. Combine dressing ingredient in separate bowl.
3. Mix salad and dressing and toss.
4. Enjoy!

SPRING BLISS LUNCH

Mushroom and Collard Greens Stir Fry

Ingredients:
2 cups collard greens, chopped
1 cup favorite mushrooms, chopped
2 cloves garlic, minced
2 tbsp. olive oil

Directions:
1. Add olive oil and garlic to frying pan.
2. Once it starts to heat up, add collards and mushrooms.
3. Sauté approximately 10 minutes.
4. Enjoy!

Apple Chard Salad

Salad Ingredients:
1 head swiss chard
1 red crunchy apple, chopped
1 cup dried sweet cherries, chopped
1 avocado
½ cup red onion

Dressing ingredients:
2 tbsp. sesame seeds, soaked (2 hours)
1 tbsp. extra virgin olive oil
1 clove garlic, minced
Juice of 2 lemons
1 pinch Himalayan sea salt

Directions:
1. Combine salad ingredients.
2. Mix dressing in separate dish.
3. Add dressing to salad mixture, toss, and enjoy.

SPRING BLISS DINNER

Quick and Yummy Sesame Kale

Ingredients:
1 bunch green or red kale, cut into bite
  size pieces
1 tbsp. olive oil
3 cloves garlic, minced
1 tbsp. soy sauce or wheat-free tamari
1 tbsp. raw honey or agave
1 tbsp. sesame oil
1 tbsp. rice vinegar
2 tbsp. toasted sesame seeds

Directions:
1. Heat large skillet or wok on medium
   heat. When hot, add the olive oil. Sauté
   garlic for 2-3 minutes.
2. Add the kale, stirring to coat all surfaces.
   Reduce heat to medium and cover.
   Cook until leaves become tender
   (about 4-6 minutes).
3. In small bowl, mix soy sauce/tamari and
   honey/agave, sesame oil and vinegar.
4. Add to kale and stir to coat evenly.
5. Remove from heat and garnish with
   sesame seeds. Enjoy!

*Tip: Try this recipe with green beans, bok
choy, or broccoli for added variety.*

Go Green with Roasted Green Beans and Shallots

Ingredients:
1 pound green beans, trimmed
3 tbsp. olive oil
4 shallots, peeled and thinly sliced
Salt and freshly ground black pepper
¼ cup slivered almonds
1/3-1/2 cup chopped fresh Italian/
  flat parsley

Directions:
1. Preheat oven to 425 ˚F.
2. Toss the green beans in a large baking
   pan with the oil and shallots and season
   with salt and pepper.
3. Roast until just cooked through and
   golden brown, about 15 to 18 minutes.
4. Combine the almonds and parsley in a
   small bowl.
5. Transfer green beans to a serving bowl
   and toss with the almond mixture.
6. Enjoy!

SPRING BLISS DINNER

Veggie Stir Fry

Ingredients:
2 carrots, thinly sliced
1 bunch broccoli
1 cup Vidalia onion, chopped
1 red pepper, chopped
1 tbsp. olive oil
1 tsp. Braggs Liquid Amino

Directions:
1. Heat oil in a large skillet or pan.
2. Add carrots and onions, stir and cook for 2 minutes.
3. Add broccoli, stir and cook for 2 minutes.
3. Add pepper and stir for 2 minutes.
4. Remove from heat, stir and leave covered for 2-3 minutes, depending on how crunchy you like your veggies.
5. Sprinkle Braggs Liquid Aminos and stir.
6. Enjoy!

Mushroom Steaks

Ingredients:
4 Portobello mushrooms
3 tsp. oregano
2 tbsp. balsamic vinegar
2 tbsp. olive oil
Himalayan sea salt and pepper, to taste

Directions:
1. Preheat oven to 350 °F.
2. Cut off mushroom stems and wash.
3. Mix oil, balsamic vinegar, oregano, and salt/pepper in a bowl.
4. Put mushroom tops in a baking dish with an edge. Pour oil mixture over mushrooms and bake for 30 minutes.
5. Enjoy!

Split Pea Soup

Ingredients:

1 frozen bag of garden peas

24 oz. vegetable broth (can us more or less for consistency)

A few dashes of fresh fennel

Himalayan sea salt, to taste

Additional spices, to taste

Directions:

1. Thaw the frozen peas overnight and chill vegetable broth.
2. Blend frozen peas, vegetable broth, and fennel in a blender until desired consistency.
3. Taste after blending and add spices accordingly.
4. Serve cold. Enjoy!

Easy Fried Rice

Ingredients:

1 small onion, chopped

1 tablespoon olive oil

2 cloves garlic, minced

1 carrot, diced

½ bunch scallion, chopped

1 tbsp. ginger, grated

4 cups cooked long grain brown rice

2 tbsp. tamari soy sauce

1 tsp. toasted sesame oil

Directions:

1. Sauté onion in olive oil for 5 minutes.
2. Add garlic and carrot and sauté for 4 minutes.
3. Add scallion and ginger and sauté for about 4 more minutes.
4. Add rice and sprinkle with water to give extra steam to dish.
5. Add tamari soy sauce and toasted sesame oil.
6. Lower heat and cool for 5 minutes more, stirring occasionally.

SPRING BLISS DINNER

Vegetarian Stuffed Peppers

Ingredients:
3 cloves garlic, crushed
Tablespoon of olive oil
Sea salt and pepper to taste
1 onion, chopped
4 large and 1 small green peppers
1 cup dry couscous, brown rice, or quinoa
One 16 oz. can stewed or chunked tomatoes
One 16 oz. can chickpeas

Directions:
1. Preheat oven to 350 °F.
2. Cook 1 cup couscous as directed and let stand for 10 minutes.
3. In large skillet, sauté onions, garlic, and small green pepper in olive oil. Add salt and pepper to taste.
4. Combine couscous, sauté mixture, stewed tomatoes, and chickpeas in a large bowl.
5. Cut the stems off the four large peppers and remove seeds.
6. Add mixture into each one of the peppers.
7. Place peppers upright in a baking dish, add a little water to the bottom and cover.
8. Bake for 45 minutes or until peppers are soft.

BONUS

For additional snack, drink and dessert recipes
for all seasons, see pages 255-265!

rock out

Play inspirational music while cooking. It will help you flow that positive, upbeat energy into the food you cook and eat.

SPRING BLISS SHOPPING LIST

Vegetables

Kale

Spinach

Swiss chard

Bok choy

Cucumbers

Collard greens

Button mushrooms

Portobello mushrooms

Tomatoes

Carrots

Onions

Celery

Assorted peppers: green, yellow, red

Frozen peas

Olives

Shallots

Scallions

Garlic

Green beans

Broccoli

Ginger

Fruits

Lemons

Bananas

Granny Smith apples

Red apples

Avocados

Strawberries

Herbs

Parsley

Cilantro

Oregano

Grains

Rolled oats
Quinoa

Other

Almond, rice or coconut milk
Almonds
Assorted nuts
Dried fruit including dried cherries, raisins, etc.
Nut butter
Vegetable broth
Chickpeas
Assorted beans

BLISS TIP

For your convenience, this list is available to download
and print at **www.BlissCleanse.com/springshoplist**

The Daily Bliss Checklist is a wonderful tool to help you stay on track each day of the two-week program. For your convenience, this list is available to download and print at www.BlissCleanse.com/checklist

DAILY **BLISS CHECKLIST**

Today's Date:_____

- ❑ Start my day with a positive thought such as: "Today is a great day!"

- ❑ Balance my body by drinking 16 oz filtered water with fresh squeezed juice of ½ lemon upon waking.

- ❑ Say my favorite affirmation(s) in front of the mirror in the morning. (Examples: "I love my body," "I am beautiful," "I live my bliss," "I am healthy, vibrant, and whole.")

- ❑ Reflect on 3-5 things I am grateful for, jotting them down in my gratitude journal, and notice how I feel when I think about them, either at morning or night.

- ❑ Choose a self-care activity for today and a time I will do it:
    - ❑ detox bath/time:_____   ❑ hot towel scrub /time:_____
    - ❑ listen to the guided meditations/time:_____   other/time:_____

- ❑ My exercise plan for the day and time I will do this:
    - ❑ walk or run/time:_____   ❑ workout at the gym/time:_____
    - ❑ yoga/exercise class/time: _____   ❑ other/time: _____   ❑ rest day

- ❑ If I'm on the go today, then pack healthy snacks such as raw nuts and seeds, cut carrots and celery, and fresh or dried fruit, along with filtered water, so I'll have them on hand when hunger strikes.

- ❑ Drink at least 64 oz. of filtered water and herbal teas. Drink even more when I can to aid the cleansing process.

- ❑ Review Today's Daily Bliss Inspiration. Try out any recommended activities that inspire me.

- ❑ Eat a healthy and satisfying breakfast, review my *Bliss Cleanse* Guidelines if necessary. Follow my Seasonal Cleansing Guides with recipes and meal plans for ideas.

- ❑ Eat a healthy mid-morning snack.

- ❑ Eat a healthy and satisfying lunch. This should be my biggest meal of the day.

- ❑ Eat a healthy afternoon snack.

- ❑ Eat a light, clean, yet satisfying dinner. Cook enough for at least two meals. My dinner should be 50% or more greens.

- ❑ One thing I appreciate about myself today: _____

- ❑ One thing I am looking forward to tomorrow: _____

- ❑ End my day with a positive thought such as, "I had a wonderful day and now I will have a wonderful rest."

- ❑ Get at least 8-9 hours of sleep.

get inspired

YOUR SPRING BLISS
DAILY INSPIRATIONS

We are so excited to bring you our daily inspirations, the **prized gem of this program!** Be sure to allow time each day to read and experience these most powerful tips.

If you feel the tendency to say, "I'll do it later," then commit now to giving yourself permission to complete each day's exercise on the day it was intended, rather than put it off, in order to fully embrace the purpose and intention of your mind-body-spirit *Bliss Cleanse*. You are worth it!!!

By following these tips each day, you will nourish yourself with the self-care needed to truly benefit from this program. Remember it's not about doing everything, it's about doing a few things each day to support you on your path to bliss.

What's great about these inspirations is that you have them to use after the cleanse is over!

Celebrate your success on taking this journey. You owe it to yourself!

Love,

Lindsey & Lorraine

DAY **ONE**

Since today is the first day of the Spring *Bliss Cleanse,* we want you to set your intentions *in writing.* Your chances of succeeding with this or any program are greatly increased when you set an intention. This helps you get clear on what you want to achieve.

So grab a journal or notebook or use the space below and let's get started!

What are you hoping to achieve from this program?

What will be the benefit to you once you have achieved it (your "WHY")?

What are ready to let go of? Perhaps you are ready to let go of a physical condition such as excess weight, tension, chronic headaches, skin problems, fatigue, or brittle hair and nails. Think about which things you are most ready to let go of. Next think about what mental or emotional conditions you want to release such as anxiety, emotional ups and downs, negativity, anger, frustration, or fear. *Write them down.*

What are you ready to bring in? Now write down a few things you are ready to bring into your life, to replace what you will be letting go. How do you want to feel come summer?

When you're finished, take a moment to thank yourself for completing today's activity!

DAY **TWO**

Today is all about gratitude!

Simply write down 3-5 things you are grateful for, and focus on how you feel
when you think about them. We recommend getting a separate journal or
notebook to do this, and practicing gratitude either first thing in the morning, or
last thing before going to bed. *From Gratitude to Bliss*® is an excellent tool to help
you begin your practice. Plan to practice gratitude every day during this cleanse
and beyond.

When you're finished, take a moment to thank yourself for completing today's activity!

DAY **THREE**

We live in such a fast-paced society, that we often forget to slow down and appreciate the moment. We not only forget to slow down and appreciate the moment, but we forget to slow down and appreciate our food.

For today, really appreciate your food for nourishing you and taking care of your body. Take time to slow down and appreciate each bite and chew. Really notice the taste, smell, color, and texture of the food before you. Think about how eating spring foods such as greens and strawberries helps you stay in tune with the season. Put your fork down after every bite. Breathe, be silent, and give thanks.

Write down any differences you notice. Is this something you can work on incorporating on a daily basis?

When you're finished, take a moment to thank yourself for completing today's activity!

DAY **FOUR**

"What we think about ourselves becomes the
truth for us ... Every thought we think is creating our
future. Each one of us creates our experiences by our
thoughts and our feelings. The thoughts we think and
the words we speak create our experiences."

–Louise Hay, *You Can Heal Your Life*[1]

**How are you talking to yourself today? Are you lifting yourself up or are
you tearing yourself down?**

Pay extra attention to how you are talking to yourself. Notice when you say
something negative and try to replace it with something positive instead.

For example, if you find yourself saying, "It's just so hard for me to lose weight."
Instead say, " I love my body and it's easy to lose weight."

It may sound silly at first, but over time, you will start thinking better and
feeling better!

When you're finished, take a moment to thank yourself for completing today's activity!

[1] Hay, Louise. You Can Heal Your Life. New York: Hay House, 1984.

DAY **FIVE**

Are you being present in day-to-day situations?

Start by simply being present in your own life. Find peace and joy in nature and your surroundings. Smile at someone walking down the hall or the sidewalk. Simply put, just be.

Appreciate the current moment for what it is, right now. Make it a discipline to stop and appreciate each moment in your life.

Challenge yourself with this exercise:

Take a mindful walk and ...

- Walk slowly.

- Stop.

- Look at the intricate details in your surroundings. What changes have you noticed now that it's spring?

- See the veins on leaves, the insects crawling on trees, and the different colors in front of you.

- Now hear the birds chirping, the wind blowing in the background, or the crinkle of leaves beneath animal feet.

- Stop once again. Would you have noticed these things if you had not made the effort to be present?

When you're finished, take a moment to thank yourself for completing today's activity!

DAY **SIX**

You're almost halfway through the mind-body-spirit *Bliss Cleanse* and you are doing an amazing job! When you give your body time to rest and replenish, you start feeling so much better!

Because we are all bio-individually different, however, we all respond to cleansing differently at first.

Pay attention to how are you feeling this week—emotionally and physically. Are you more energetic and happy? Or are you more lethargic and moody?

Pay attention to how your body is feeling and reacting. Journal your thoughts!

When you're finished, take a moment to thank yourself for completing today's activity!

DAY **SEVEN**

It's one thing to eat healthy and cleanse yourself physically, but it is also just as important to cleanse yourself emotionally.

Often times, we let past wounds take foot in our lives and shape us into someone we are not. So instead of dwelling, we want you to list all the reasons why you are amazing! Shifting from a negative to a positive light can not only spread happiness, but it can also shed "weight" we have been carrying around for years.

Why are YOU amazing? What qualities make you amazing, inside and out?

Embrace those qualities by recording them below. When you aren't feeling so good about yourself, look back on your list and remember all your beautiful qualities.

I am amazing because:

When you're finished, take a moment to thank yourself for completing today's activity!

DAY **EIGHT**

You're halfway there! WOOO-HOOO! Way to go! Stop and appreciate this success and the other successes along the way.

We are always trying to get to an end result, and we often dismiss the small successes along the way. Stop and appreciate the successes you had just this morning: making yourself a delish breakfast, taking the kids to school, or sending out a birthday card.

You have accomplished a week-long cleanse! That is a huge success in itself! What other successes have you noticed this week? Take a moment to reflect on all the good that has happened this past week. Write them down!

My recent successes:

When you're finished, take a moment to thank yourself for completing today's activity!

DAY **NINE**

Take some time and focus on stretching today – whether it is in the morning, at your work desk, at a meeting, etc.

Take some time to do some simple stretches to get your blood flowing!

Stretching not only increases your flexibility and helps relieve pain, but it can also generate better blood circulation which helps brings nutrients to your cells AND flushes out toxins. So really, it's a win-win!

Get stretching!

When you're finished, take a moment to thank yourself for completing today's activity!

DAY **TEN**

It's no secret that regular exercise is good for you. It's not only important to try light exercises that help you stretch and strengthen, but it's also important to try exercises that help you break a sweat! Sweating helps release built up toxins and also helps tighten your skin!

Not there yet? Listen to your body and take it slow. If you're feeling a little tired, get outside and walk! A 10-minute walk is enough to increase energy and improve mood for up to two hours!

When you're finished, take a moment to thank yourself for completing today's activity!

DAY **ELEVEN**

Focus on spreading your love and light into the world by paying it forward. Focus today on doing small things for others. These small things could make a huge difference in someone's life!

Here are some suggestions to get you started, but remember to use your creativity and make this practice authentic to you! Use the space at the end to add your own ideas. Try something new with each season.

- Buy a stranger coffee when you find yourself waiting in line
- Put a quarter in a meter that is about to expire
- Smile at a stranger
- Tip a server generously
- Donate to your favorite charity
- Compliment someone in the checkout line
- Volunteer at a local shelter
- Hold the door for someone
- Offer advice to a friend
- Invite someone to cut in front of you at the grocery store
- Donate blood
- _____

- _____

- _____

- _____

- _____

When you're finished, take a moment to thank yourself for completing today's activity!

DAY **TWELVE**

Take some time out today to focus on meditation. Meditation is a way to let go of outside stressors and key in on what's really important!

Practice Easy Meditation: Take a 5-15 minute break every day, close your eyes and focus on your breath. Breathe in something you are grateful for. Breathe out any stress you may be feeling in your body. If your mind wanders, simply bring it back to your breath.

Also check out the *Bliss Meditation Collection* for a guided approach to getting started, available at **www.BlissCleanse.com/shop.**

When you're finished, take a moment to thank yourself for completing today's activity!

DAY **THIRTEEN**

Cleansing in all areas is really important. We have been working on the body and the mind, but today let's look at your space!

Out with the old; in with the new! "Spring" cleaning can be the most cleansing act of them all and can be done with each season! Whether it's sorting through and clearing out old clothes, organizing your closets and kitchen cabinets, or finishing incomplete projects, cleaning up is a refreshing and feel-good process. Hello, peace of mind!

Start small with one space or room and work your way up! You will be complete before you know it! And remember—it's not a race!

If this seems too overwhelming, simply aim to de-clutter at least one area of your home—a room, a closet, or your files—with each season.

When you're finished, take a moment to thank yourself for completing today's activity!

DAY **FOURTEEN**

Congratulations!

Today is the last day of your *Bliss Spring Cleanse!* Stop and savor your success in taking this amazing journey to your health and happiness. Reflect on the areas you want to continue with and set your intentions moving forward.

Honor those intentions. Move forward blissfully. And remember that small changes lead to big results!

Woo-hoo!
Way to go!!!

take note

Use the pages that follow to make notes during the Spring *Bliss Cleanse.* These will prove helpful when you return this summer!

TODAY'S DATE:

What I found helpful...

What I found challenging...

TODAY'S DATE:

· ·

What I want to work on next time...

Recipes I want to try next time...

TODAY'S DATE:

· ·

TODAY'S DATE:

TODAY'S DATE:

TODAY'S DATE:

· ·

TODODAY'S DATE:

· ·

TODAY'S DATE:

. . . .

TODAY'S DATE:

· ·

TODAY'S DATE:

. . . .

SUMMER
BLISS
CLEANSING GUIDE

On the following pages you'll find a suggested meal plan, healthy and delicious recipes, a shopping list, a daily checklist, and daily inspirations – everything you need to cleanse during summer months!

SUMMER BLISS MEAL PLAN

	DAY 1	DAY 2	DAY 3
Morning Bliss	List 5 things you are grateful for	List 5 things you are grateful for	List 5 things you are grateful for
AM Detox Water	Drink 1 glass of water (or cup of hot water) with fresh squeezed juice of ½ lemon	Drink 1 glass of water (or cup of hot water) with fresh squeezed juice of ½ lemon	Drink 1 glass of water (or cup of hot water) with fresh squeezed juice of ½ lemon
Breakfast	Greek Yogurt with Blueberries and Almonds	Oatmeal Smoothie	Berry-Liscious Smoothie
AM Snack	Fresh fruit	A few pieces of dry seaweed	Handful of almonds
Lunch	Sautéed Veggies with Quinoa	Leftover Sautéed Veggies with Quinoa	Minty Cucumber Salad
Mid-Day Snack	Mixed Veggies and Hummus	Handful of Pumpkin Seeds	Handful of Sugar Snap Peas
Dinner	Romaine Lettuce Wraps	Black Bean Tacos	Peruvian Quinoa Salad
Night-time Bliss	What's one positive thing that happened today?	List 3 successes that happened today.	Take a mindful walk after dinner.

DAY 4	DAY 5	DAY 6	DAY 7
List 5 things you are grateful for	List 5 things you are grateful for	List 5 things you are grateful for	List 5 things you are grateful for
Drink 1 glass of water (or cup of hot water) with fresh squeezed juice of ½ lemon	Drink 1 glass of water (or cup of hot water) with fresh squeezed juice of ½ lemon	Drink 1 glass of water (or cup of hot water) with fresh squeezed juice of ½ lemon	Drink 1 glass of water (or cup of hot water) with fresh squeezed juice of ½ lemon
Greek Yogurt with Blueberries and Almonds	Bliss Green Smoothie	Chovocado Smoothie	Bliss Green Smoothie
Fresh berries	Plum	Celery and almond Butter	Rice cake (plain or with nut butter)
Leftover Peruvian Quinoa Salad	Spinach and Strawberry Salad	Romaine Lettuce Wraps	Black Bean and Pepper Salad
Tortilla Chips + Salsa	Coconut Water Rice Pudding	Plain Yogurt with Grapefruit	Plain Popcorn
Sautéed Veggies with Quinoa	Edamame, Carrot, and Seaweed Rice	Guacamole Pita	Spinach and Strawberry Salad
Give yourself a hot towel scrub at night.	Make something handmade and give it to a friend!	Take a lavender bubble bath.	Make some ginger tea for comfort.

SUMMER BLISS BREAKFAST

Greek Yogurt with Blueberries and Almonds

Ingredients:
Plain Greek yogurt
½ cup blueberries
Handful of almonds

Directions
1. Add Greek yogurt to a bowl
2. Add blueberries and almonds
3. Enjoy!

Oatmeal Smoothie
Ingredients:

½ cup cooked oats
½ cup fresh strawberries
1 banana
½ cup almond milk

Blend ingredients and enjoy!

Berry-Licious Smoothie

Ingredients:
½ cup strawberries
¼ cup blueberries
¼ cup raspberries
¼ cup almond or rice milk
A handful of ice

Blend ingredients and enjoy!

BLISS TIP

Give your smoothie some added detox action with chia seeds. Chia seeds are a superfood that absorbs toxins in the intestinal tract and keeps your colon clean.

Bliss Green Smoothie

Ingredients:
½ cup of your choice chopped greens
    (spinach, kale, dandelion, or another
    favorite green)
1 banana
½ cup almond or rice milk

Blend ingredients and enjoy!

Chocovado Smoothie

Ingredients:
1 avocado
1 banana (preferably frozen)
½ cup almond or rice milk
1 tbsp. raw cacao powder

Directions:
1. Blend well in blender.
2. Add ice for a thicker texture.
3. Serve immediately.

BLISS TIP

Create your own "super smoothies." Add superfoods to your smoothies such as raw cacao, maca powder, bee pollen, spirulina powder, or hemp seed, for added health benefits. *See pages 57-59 for more info!*

SUMMER BLISS LUNCH

Spinach and Strawberry Salad

Salad Ingredients:
5 cups of fresh baby spinach
1 ½ cups of strawberries, sliced
½ cup of walnuts, crushed

Lemon Drop Dressing Ingredients:
3 tbsp. of fresh lemon juice
¼ cup olive oil
2 tsp. honey
1 bunch finely chopped fresh basil

Directions:
1. Combine salad ingredients in a large bowl.
2. Prepare salad dressing in a small bowl.
3. Pour dressing over salad and enjoy!

Minty Cucumber Salad

Ingredients:
1 cucumber
1 green apple
1 handful fresh mint
Sea salt
Juice of ½ lemon

Directions:
1. Thinly slice the cucumbers and apple.
2. Rub the salt into the slices.
3. Finely chop the mint and mix it into the salad.
4. Add the lemon juice on top and mix.
5. Enjoy!

BLISS TIP

Cook once, eat twice. A great way to leverage your cleanse is to cook enough food so that you can eat twice. For example, turn your dinner into tomorrow's lunch.

Sautéed Veggies with Quinoa

Ingredients:
1 zucchini
1 yellow squash
1 red pepper
½ red onion
3 garlic cloves, chopped
2-3 tbsp. olive oil
Sea salt
1 cup quinoa, cooked

Directions:
1. Prepare quinoa as directed.
2. Cut up zucchini, yellow squash, red pepper and onion.
3. Add oil and garlic to frying pan.
4. Add veggies and grill for 15-20 minutes or until tender.
5. Prepare veggies with a side of quinoa.
6. Enjoy!

Black Bean and Red Pepper Salad

Bean Salad Ingredients:
One 16 oz. can black beans, drained and rinsed
1 red bell pepper, diced
1 green pepper, diced
1 cup thinly sliced celery
1 cup thinly sliced green onions

Cilantro-Cumin Dressing:
¼ cup chopped, fresh cilantro
5 tbsp. olive oil
¼ cup red wine vinegar
1 tsp. ground cumin

Directions:
1. Combine the beans, peppers, celery, and green onions in a large mixing bowl.
2. Whisk the oil, vinegar, cumin, and chopped cilantro in a smaller, separate bowl.
3. Pour the dressing over the vegetables and stir until thoroughly coated.
4. Let stand 15 minutes to blend the flavors, or refrigerate up to 2 hours before serving.
5. To serve, spoon the salad onto a bed of lettuce or greens. Enjoy!

SUMMER BLISS DINNER

Romaine Lettuce Wraps

Ingredients:
2 large romaine leaves
1 shredded carrot
Handful of alfalfa sprouts
Red onion, sliced and cut into
    small pieces
Hummus (see p. 256) or
    guacamole (p172)
Black pepper and sea salt to taste

Directions:
1. Wash and flatten romaine leaves.
2. Spread center area with hummus or guacamole.
3. Layer carrots, onions and sprouts.
4. Add salt and pepper.
5. Fold edges of leaves to make a wrap.

Black Bean Tacos

Ingredients:
1 can black beans, drained and rinsed
1 red bell pepper, diced
1 small onion, diced
½ cup fresh cilantro
2 tbsp. olive oil
2 soft corn tortilla shells

Directions:
1. Add olive oil to large skillet and heat.
2. Add peppers, onions, and cilantro. Sauté 5 minutes.
3. Add black beans, sauté 15 minutes.
4. Heat up corn tortilla in a skillet or the oven.
5. Add black bean mixture to a tortilla and enjoy!

BLISS TIP

Detox with apple cider vinegar. Did you know apple cider vinegar makes a great cleansing digestive aid and also a great facial toner? Drink one tablespoon mixed into a glass of water before meals. For a skin toner, mix one part vinegar with three or four parts water. Use cotton ball to cleanse your face.

Edamame, Carrot, and Seaweed Rice

Ingredients:
1 cup edamame beans
2 carrots, diced
3 sheets dried seaweed
3 garlic cloves, chopped
1 cup brown rice
2 tbsp. olive oil
1 tsp. sea salt
1 tbsp. sesame oil

Directions:
1. Prepare brown rice as directed.
2. In a large skillet, add olive oil and garlic. Sauté 5 minutes.
3. Add carrots and edamame beans and heat on medium for 5-10 minutes.
4. Tear seaweed into small pieces, add to the stir fry, and continue cooking on medium heat for 5 minutes.
5. Add cooked brown rice, sesame oil, and continue cooking on medium heat for 10-15 minutes or until rice is browned.
6. Remove from heat, let cool, and serve.

Peruvian Quinoa Salad

Ingredients:
1 cup dry quinoa
½ cup scallions
1 red pepper, diced
2 Roma tomatoes, diced
1 cucumber, diced
¼ cup pine nuts
½ cup dry cranberries

Dressing:
5 tbsp. olive oil
3 bunches chopped parsley
Juice of 1 lemon
1 tsp. maple syrup

Directions:
1. Cook 1 cup quinoa as directed and let cool.
2. Dice all vegetables and place to the side.
3. Prepare dressing and place to the side.
4. Take a small skillet and roast the ¼ cup pine nuts for 5 minutes
5. Add quinoa, vegetables, cranberries and pine nuts to one bowl.
6. Add dressing and mix. Refrigerate for up to two hours.
7. Enjoy!

SUMMER BLISS DINNER

Guacamole Pita

Homemade Guacamole

Ingredients:
4 ripe avocados
Juice of 1 lime
3 cloves garlic, minced
1 small onion, finely chopped
1 tomato
½ cup cilantro, chopped
Sea salt
Freshly ground pepper

Directions:
1. Slice tomato in half, remove the seeds and dice.
2. Cut avocados in half and remove the pits, saving them for later.
3. With a large spoon, scoop out avocados and place in medium bowl.
4. With a fork, mash avocados until smooth, leaving small chunks if desired.
5. Add lime juice, onions, tomatoes, garlic and cilantro, stirring together gently.
6. Add salt and pepper to taste.
7. Place pits in bowl and chill for 30 minutes.
8. Transfer to small bowl and garnish with cilantro.

Guacamole Pita

Ingredients:
3 tbsp. homemade guacamole
1 pita
½ cup spinach
2 slices of tomato
handful of sprouts

Directions:
1. Spread guacamole inside pita.
2. Add spinach, tomato, and sprouts.
3. Enjoy!

Experiment with spices. Spices are a great way to add flavor, flare, and nutrition to every meal. Don't be afraid to add a few dashes of something new!

spice it up

For additional snack, drink and dessert recipes for all seasons, see page 255-265!

SUMMER BLISS SHOPPING LIST

Vegetables

Spinach
Cucumbers
Zucchini
Yellow squash
Assorted peppers: green, yellow, red
Garlic
Onions
Celery
Romaine lettuce
Carrots
Sprouts
Edamame beans
Scallions
Tomatoes

Fruits

Lemons
Blueberries
Bananas
Strawberries
Raspberries
Blackberries
Avocado
Green apples
Plums

Herbs

Mint
Cilantro

Grains

Rolled oats
Quinoa
Brown rice

Other

Unsweetened Greek yogurt
Almonds
Almond, rice or coconut milk
Raw cacao
Walnuts
Black beans
Chickpeas
Corn tortilla shells
Pine nuts
Dried cranberries (unsweetened)

BLISS TIP

For your convenience, this list is available to download and print at **www.BlissCleanse.com/summershoplist**

The Daily Bliss Checklist is a wonderful tool to help you stay on track each day of the two-week program. For your convenience, this list is available to download and print at www.BlissCleanse.com/checklist

focus

DAILY **BLISS CHECKLIST**

Today's Date:_____

❑ Start my day with a positive thought such as: "Today is a great day!"

❑ Balance my body by drinking 16 oz filtered water with fresh squeezed juice of ½ lemon upon waking.

❑ Say my favorite affirmation(s) in front of the mirror in the morning. (Examples: "I love my body," "I am beautiful," "I live my bliss," "I am healthy, vibrant, and whole.")

❑ Reflect on 3-5 things I am grateful for, jotting them down in my gratitude journal, and notice how I feel when I think about them, either at morning or night.

❑ Choose a self-care activity for today and a time I will do it:
   ❑ detox bath/time:_____   ❑ hot towel scrub /time: _____
   ❑ listen to the guided meditations/time:_____   other/time:_____

❑ My exercise plan for the day and time I will do this:
   ❑ walk or run/time:_____   ❑ workout at the gym/time:_____
   ❑ yoga/exercise class/time: _____   ❑ other/time: _____   ❑ rest day

❑ If I'm on the go today, then pack healthy snacks such as raw nuts and seeds, cut carrots and celery, and fresh or dried fruit, along with filtered water, so I'll have them on hand when hunger strikes.

❑ Drink at least 64 oz. of filtered water and herbal teas. Drink even more when I can to aid the cleansing process.

❑ Review Today's Daily Bliss Inspiration. Try out any recommended activities that inspire me.

❑ Eat a healthy and satisfying breakfast, review my *Bliss Cleanse* Guidelines if necessary. Follow my Seasonal Cleansing Guides with recipes and meal plans for ideas.

❑ Eat a healthy mid-morning snack.

❑ Eat a healthy and satisfying lunch. This should be my biggest meal of the day.

❑ Eat a healthy afternoon snack.

❑ Eat a light, clean, yet satisfying dinner. Cook enough for at least two meals. My dinner should be 50% or more greens.

❑ One thing I appreciate about myself today: _____

❑ One thing I am looking forward to tomorrow: _____

❑ End my day with a positive thought such as, "I had a wonderful day and now I will have a wonderful rest."

❑ Get at least 8-9 hours of sleep.

get inspired

YOUR SUMMER BLISS
DAILY INSPIRATIONS

We are so excited to bring you our daily inspirations, the **prized gem of this program!** Be sure to allow time each day to read and experience these most powerful tips.

If you feel the tendency to say, "I'll do it later," then commit now to giving yourself permission to complete each day's exercise on the day it was intended, rather than put it off, in order to fully embrace the purpose and intention of your mind-body-spirit *Bliss Cleanse*. You are worth it!!!

By following these tips each day, you will nourish yourself with the self-care needed to truly benefit from this program. Remember it's not about doing everything, it's about doing a few things each day to support you on your path to bliss.

What's great about these inspirations is that you have them to use after the cleanse is over!

Celebrate your success on taking this journey. You owe it to yourself!

Love,

Lindsey & Lorraine

DAY **ONE**

Since today is the first day of the Summer *Bliss Cleanse,* we want you to set your intentions *in writing.* Your chances of succeeding with this or any program are greatly increased when you set an intention. This helps you get clear on what you want to achieve.

So grab a journal or notebook or use the space below and let's get started!

What are you hoping to achieve from this program?

What will be the benefit to you once you have achieved it (your "WHY")?

What are ready to let go of? Perhaps you are ready to let go of a physical condition such as excess weight, tension, chronic headaches, skin problems, fatigue, or brittle hair and nails. Think about which things you are most ready to let go of. Next think about what mental or emotional conditions you want to release such as anxiety, emotional ups and downs, negativity, anger, frustration, or fear. *Write them down.*

What are you ready to bring in? Now write down a few things you are ready to bring into your life, to replace what you will be letting go. How do you want to feel come fall?

When you're finished, take a moment to thank yourself for completing today's activity!

DAY **TWO**

Today is all about gratitude!

Simply write down 3-5 things you are grateful for, and focus on how you feel when you think about them. We recommend getting a separate journal or notebook to do this, and practicing gratitude either first thing in the morning, or last thing before going to bed. *From Gratitude to Bliss®* is an excellent tool to help you begin your practice. Plan to practice gratitude every day during this cleanse and beyond.

When you're finished, take a moment to thank yourself for completing today's activity!

DAY **THREE**

We live in such a fast-paced society, that we often forget to slow down and appreciate the moment. We not only forget to slow down and appreciate the moment, but we forget to slow down and appreciate our food.

For today, really appreciate your food for nourishing you and taking care of your body. Take time to slow down and appreciate each bite and chew. Really notice the taste, smell, color, and texture of the food before you. Think about how eating summer foods such as melons and berries help you stay in tune with the season. Put your fork down after every bite. Breathe, be silent, and give thanks.

Write down any differences you notice. Is this something you can work on incorporating on a daily basis?

When you're finished, take a moment to thank yourself for completing today's activity!

DAY **FOUR**

"What we think about ourselves becomes the
truth for us ... Every thought we think is creating our
future. Each one of us creates our experiences by our
thoughts and our feelings. The thoughts we think and
the words we speak create our experiences."

–Louise Hay, *You Can Heal Your Life*[1]

How are you talking to yourself today? Are you lifting yourself up or are you tearing yourself down?

Pay extra attention to how you are talking to yourself. Notice when you say something negative and try to replace it with something positive instead.

For example, if you find yourself saying, "It's just so hard for me to lose weight." Instead say, " I love my body and it's easy to lose weight."

It may sound silly at first, but over time, you will start thinking better and feeling better!

When you're finished, take a moment to thank yourself for completing today's activity!

[1] Hay, Louise. You Can Heal Your Life. New York: Hay House, 1984.

DAY **FIVE**

Are you being present in day-to-day situations?

Start by simply being present in your own life. Find peace and joy in nature and your surroundings. Smile at someone walking down the hall or the sidewalk. Simply put, just be.

Appreciate the current moment for what it is, right now. Make it a discipline to stop and appreciate each moment in your life.

Challenge yourself with this exercise:

Take a mindful walk and ...

- Walk slowly.
- Stop.
- Look at the intricate details in your surroundings. What changes have you noticed now that it's summer?
- See the veins on leaves, the insects crawling on trees, and the different colors in front of you.
- Now hear the birds chirping, the wind blowing in the background, or the crinkle of leaves beneath animal feet.
- Stop once again. Would you have noticed these things if you had not made the effort to be present?

When you're finished, take a moment to thank yourself for completing today's activity!

DAY **SIX**

You're almost halfway through the mind-body-spirit *Bliss Cleanse* and you are doing an amazing job! When you give your body time to rest and replenish, you start feeling so much better!

Because we are all bio-individually different, however, we all respond to cleansing differently at first.

Pay attention to how are you feeling this week—emotionally and physically. Are you more energetic and happy? Or are you more lethargic and moody?

Pay attention to how your body is feeling and reacting. Journal your thoughts!

When you're finished, take a moment to thank yourself for completing today's activity!

DAY **SEVEN**

It's one thing to eat healthy and cleanse yourself physically, but it is also just as important to cleanse yourself emotionally.

Often times, we let past wounds take foot in our lives and shape us into someone we are not. So instead of dwelling, we want you to list all the reasons why you are amazing! Shifting from a negative to a positive light can not only spread happiness, but it can also shed "weight" we have been carrying around for years.

Why are YOU amazing? What qualities make you amazing, inside and out?

Embrace those qualities by recording them below. When you aren't feeling so good about yourself, look back on your list and remember all your beautiful qualities.

I am amazing because:

When you're finished, take a moment to thank yourself for completing today's activity!

DAY **EIGHT**

You're halfway there! WOOO-HOOO! Way to go! Stop and appreciate this success and the other successes along the way.

We are always trying to get to an end result, and we often dismiss the small successes along the way. Stop and appreciate the successes you had just this morning: making yourself a delish breakfast, taking the kids to school, or sending out a birthday card.

You have accomplished a week-long cleanse! That is a huge success in itself! What other successes have you noticed this week? Take a moment to reflect on all the good that has happened this past week. Write them down!

My recent successes:

When you're finished, take a moment to thank yourself for completing today's activity!

DAY **NINE**

Take some time and focus on stretching today – whether it is in the morning, at your work desk, at a meeting, etc.

Take some time to do some simple stretches to get your blood flowing!

Stretching not only increases your flexibility and helps relieve pain, but it can also generate better blood circulation which helps brings nutrients to your cells AND flushes out toxins. So really, it's a win-win!

Get stretching!

When you're finished, take a moment to thank yourself for completing today's activity!

DAY **TEN**

It's no secret that regular exercise is good for you. It's not only important to try light exercises that help you stretch and strengthen, but it's also important to try exercises that help you break a sweat! Sweating helps release built up toxins and also helps tighten your skin!

Not there yet? Listen to your body and take it slow. If you're feeling a little tired, get outside and walk! A 10-minute walk is enough to increase energy and improve mood for up to two hours!

When you're finished, take a moment to thank yourself for completing today's activity!

DAY **ELEVEN**

Focus on spreading your love and light into the world by paying it forward. Focus today on doing small things for others. These small things could make a huge difference in someone's life!

Here are some suggestions to get you started, but remember to use your creativity and make this practice authentic to you! Use the space at the end to add your own ideas. Try something new with each season.

* Buy a stranger coffee when you find yourself waiting in line
* Put a quarter in a meter that is about to expire
* Smile at a stranger
* Tip a server generously
* Donate to your favorite charity
* Compliment someone in the checkout line
* Volunteer at a local shelter
* Hold the door for someone
* Offer advice to a friend
* Invite someone to cut in front of you at the grocery store
* Donate blood
* _____

* _____

* _____

* _____

* _____

When you're finished, take a moment to thank yourself for completing today's activity!

DAY **TWELVE**

Take some time out today to focus on meditation. Meditation is a way to let go of outside stressors and key in on what's really important!

Practice Easy Meditation: Take a 5-15 minute break every day, close your eyes and focus on your breath. Breathe in something you are grateful for. Breathe out any stress you may be feeling in your body. If your mind wanders, simply bring it back to your breath.

Also check out the *Bliss Meditation Collection* for a guided approach to getting started, available at **www.BlissCleanse.com/shop.**

When you're finished, take a moment to thank yourself for completing today's activity!

DAY **THIRTEEN**

Cleansing in all areas is really important. We have been working on the body and the mind, but today let's look at your space!

Out with the old; in with the new! "Spring" cleaning can be the most cleansing act of them all and can be done with each season! Whether it's sorting through and clearing out old clothes, organizing your closets and kitchen cabinets, or finishing incomplete projects, cleaning up is a refreshing and feel-good process. Hello, peace of mind!

Start small with one space or room and work your way up! You will be complete before you know it! And remember—it's not a race!

If this seems too overwhelming, simply aim to de-clutter at least one area of your home—a room, a closet, or your files—with each season.

When you're finished, take a moment to thank yourself for completing today's activity!

DAY **FOURTEEN**

Congratulations!

Today is the last day of your *Bliss Summer Cleanse!* Stop and savor your success in taking this amazing journey to your health and happiness. Reflect on the areas you want to continue with and set your intentions moving forward.

Honor those intentions. Move forward blissfully. And remember that small changes lead to big results!

Woo-hoo!
Way to go!!!

take note

BLISS TIP

Use the pages that follow to make notes during the Summer *Bliss Cleanse.* These will prove helpful when you return this fall!

TODAY'S DATE:

What I found helpful...

What I found challenging...

TODAY'S DATE:

· ·

What I want to work on next time...

Recipes I want to try next time...

TODAY'S DATE:

· ·

TODAY'S DATE:

TODAY'S DATE:

TODAY'S DATE:

TODAY'S DATE:

TODAY'S DATE:

· ·

TODAY'S DATE:

....

TODAY'S DATE:

. . . .

FALL BLISS

CLEANSING GUIDE

On the following pages you'll find a suggested meal plan, healthy and delicious recipes, a shopping list, a daily checklist and daily, inspirations – everything you need to cleanse during fall months!

FALL BLISS MEAL PLAN

	DAY 1	DAY 2	DAY 3
Morning Bliss	List 5 things you are grateful for	List 5 things you are grateful for	List 5 things you are grateful for
AM Detox Water	Drink 1 glass of water (or cup of hot water) with fresh squeezed juice of ½ lemon	Drink 1 glass of water (or cup of hot water) with fresh squeezed juice of ½ lemon	Drink 1 glass of water (or cup of hot water) with fresh squeezed juice of ½ lemon
Breakfast	Bliss Green Smoothie	Pumpkin Pie Pancakes	Pumpkin Pie Smoothie
AM Snack	Peppers and Hummus	An Apple	Handful of Almonds
Lunch	Apples with Pecans and Raw Honey	Leftover Protein Power Spiced Quinoa	Creamy Coconut Pumpkin Soup
Mid-Day Snack	Cucumber Sliders	Handful of Pumpkin Seeds	Handful of Sugar Snap Peas
Dinner	Protein Power Spiced Quinoa	Spaghetti Squash with Parsley and Cinnamon	Quinoa with Roasted Root Vegetables
Night-time Bliss	What's one positive thing that happened today?	List 3 successes that happened today.	Take a mindful walk after dinner.

DAY 4	DAY 5	DAY 6	DAY 7
List 5 things you are grateful for	List 5 things you are grateful for	List 5 things you are grateful for	List 5 things you are grateful for
Drink 1 glass of water (or cup of hot water) with fresh squeezed juice of ½ lemon	Drink 1 glass of water (or cup of hot water) with fresh squeezed juice of ½ lemon	Drink 1 glass of water (or cup of hot water) with fresh squeezed juice of ½ lemon	Drink 1 glass of water (or cup of hot water) with fresh squeezed juice of ½ lemon
Bliss Energizer	Type A Smoothie	I'm in Love Smoothie	2 Mini Veggie Muffins
Fresh berries	Pomegranate Juice	Celery and almond butter	Rice cake (plain or with nut butter)
Roasted Veggie Soup	Roasted Veggie Wrap	Quick and Simple Pear Salad	Mushroom Wrap
Mini Veggie Muffins	Handful of almonds	Apples with Pecans, Almond Butter and Raw Honey	Popcorn with sea salt and crushed walnuts
Roasted Brussels Sprouts and Brown Rice	Veggie Burger	Sweet Potato Quesadilla	Veggie Bake
Give yourself a hot towel scrub at night.	Make something handmade and give it to a friend!	Take a lavender bubble bath.	Make some ginger tea for comfort.

FALL BLISS BREAKFAST

Bliss Green Smoothie

Ingredients:
½ cup of your choice chopped greens
    (spinach, kale, dandelion, or another
    favorite green)
1 banana
½ cup almond or rice milk

Blend ingredients and enjoy!

Bliss Energizer

Ingredients:
1 bunch of kale, finely chopped
2 carrots
1 cucumber
1 lemon

Directions:
1. Juice all ingredients with a juicer.
2. Enjoy!

*Note: add a slice of ginger to the juice or a
dash of cayenne pepper for an added kick.*

Mini Veggie Muffins

Ingredients:
1 cup veggies, grated or finely chopped
    (suggestions: carrots, zucchini, squash,
    peppers, onions)
2 eggs, beaten
2 cups quinoa or spelt flour
½ cup parsley, finely chopped
1 cup soy or rice milk
Pinch of sea salt

Directions:
1. Preheat oven to 325 °F.
2. Mix flour and salt in a bowl.
3. Make a well, add eggs, veggies
   and parsley.
4. Mix lightly, gradually add milk. This is
   supposed to be lumpy so don't work
   too hard!
5. Spoon into a mini muffin tray that is
   lightly oiled.
6. Bake for 12-15 minutes.
7. Remove and allow to set for 10
   minutes, then serve.

Type A Smoothie

Ingredients:
½ cup frozen, unsweetened
  pineapple chunks
1 banana
½ cup kale
½ cup coconut milk
1 tbsp. chia seeds
2 ice cubes

Directions:
1. Blend all ingredients except the
  chia seeds.
2. Pour smoothie into a cup and sprinkle
  chia seeds on top
3. Enjoy!

Pumpkin Pie Smoothie
Serves 2

Ingredients:
1 peeled and frozen banana
½ cup pumpkin, canned
¾ cup unsweetened almond milk
1 tsp. pumpkin pie spice
2 tsp. cinnamon
1 tsp. vanilla
1 tbsp. honey (optional)

Blend all ingredients and enjoy!

BLISS TIP

Create your own "super smoothies." Add superfoods to your smoothies such as raw cacao, maca powder, bee pollen, spirulina powder, or hemp seed, for added health benefits. *See pages 57-59 for more info!*

FALL BLISS BREAKFAST

I'm in Love Smoothie

Ingredients:
8 pitted sweet bing cherries (fresh or
    frozen)
1 banana
2 tbsp. dark chocolate or
    carob chips
½ cup of unsweetened vanilla
    almond milk

Directions:
Blend all ingredients well in blender.
Add more ice for a thicker texture.
Serve immediately.

Pumpkin Pie Pancakes

Ingredients:
1 ½ cup oatmeal
½ cup whole wheat flour or almond flour
2 tsp. baking powder
2 tsp. cinnamon or pumpkin
    pie spice
½ cup canned pumpkin
1 ¼ cup almond or rice milk

Directions:
1. Mix dry ingredients together in a
    medium size mixing bowl.
2. Add almond milk and mix.
3. Add pumpkin to mixture.
4. Lightly grease pan with olive or
    coconut oil and turn on medium heat.
5. Pour batter into small round pancakes
    and heat until batter is fully cooked or
    when sides are golden brown.
6. Enjoy!

BLISS TIP

Give your smoothie some added detox action with chia seeds. Chia seeds are a superfood that absorbs toxins in the intestinal tract and keeps your colon clean.

FALL BLISS LUNCH

Creamy Coconut Pumpkin Soup

Ingredients:
1 tbsp. olive oil
1 large onion, chopped
3 garlic cloves, minced
1 large pumpkin flesh, chopped
3 carrots, chopped
3 tbsp. rosemary
4 cups vegetable broth
3 bay leaves
1 cup coconut milk
Himalayan sea salt, to taste
Pepper, to taste

Directions:
1. In large saucepan, heat olive oil, garlic, and onions. Sauté on medium for 3-4 minutes.
2. Add pumpkin, carrots, and rosemary. Sauté for another 3-4 minutes.
3. Add vegetable broth and bay leaves.
4. Bring to the boil, cover, and simmer for 15-20 minutes or until vegetables are tender. Remove bay leaves. Let cool.
6. Place half the soup in a large blender and add ½ cup coconut milk. Blend together.
7. Pour into a large bowl.
8. Repeat remaining soup and coconut milk.
9. Pour all of the soup back into the saucepan. Add salt and pepper to taste. Heat for 10-12 minutes, mixing as needed.
10. Remove from heat and serve. Enjoy!

Apples with Pecans, Almond Butter and Raw Honey

Ingredients:
1 or 2 organic apples
1 tbsp. almond butter
½ cup pecans, chopped
Sprinkle of cinnamon
Sprinkle of nutmeg
1 tbsp. raw honey

Directions:
1. Half and core the apple(s).
2. Make very thin slices and fan out onto a serving plate.
3. Spread almond butter on top of apple slices and top with pecans.
4. Sprinkle with spices.
5. Drizzle honey.
6. Eat and enjoy!

FALL BLISS LUNCH

Roasted Veggie Soup

Ingredients:
5 carrots, chopped
1 sweet onion, chopped
5 celery stalks, chopped
5-6 cloves garlic, chopped
2 tbsp. olive oil
8 cups vegetable broth
3 bay leaves
2 cups wild rice
Himalayan sea salt, to taste
Pepper, to taste
Additional spices to taste

Directions:
1. In a large skillet, heat olive oil and gently cook garlic and onion without browning, for 3-4 minutes.
2. Add other veggies and cook for another 2-3 minutes.
3. Add vegetable broth and bay leaves to a deep pot.
4. Add veggies and wild rice to the vegetable broth.
5. Bring to boil, then cover and simmer for 60 minutes or until rice is cooked.
6. Enjoy!

Roasted Veggie Wrap

Ingredients:
Gluten-free flour tortilla
2 spoonfuls of hummus *(see recipe p256)*
Favorite fall veggies such as sweet potatoes, brussel sprouts, broccoli, etc.
Favorite spices

Directions:
1. Spoon the hummus onto the wrap.
2. Add your favorite veggies and spices.
3. Wrap and enjoy!

Mushroom Wrap

Ingredients:
Handful of mushrooms, chopped
1 carrot, chopped
½ pepper, chopped
1 tbsp. olive oil
1 tbsp. balsamic vinegar
1 large collard leaf for a wrap
Sea salt and pepper, to taste

Directions:
1. Sauté oil and balsamic vinegar with mushrooms, carrot, and pepper for 3-4 minutes until tender.
2. Lay collard leaf flat and add veggies and salt and pepper to taste. Enjoy!

Apple Choy Slaw

Salad Ingredients:
5 stalks of bok choy, chopped
1 Granny Smith apple, sliced
½ small red onion, thinly sliced

Dressing Ingredients:
2 tbsp. apple cider vinegar (or
   lemon juice)
2 tsp. honey or brown rice syrup
1 tsp. ground coriander
1 tsp. Dijon mustard
¼ cup olive oil
Juice of ½ lemon

Directions:
1. Combine all salad ingredients in a bowl.
2. Prepare dressing in a separate bowl or shaker container and mix well.
3. Pour dressing over salad.
4. Eat immediately and enjoy!

Quick & Simple Pear Salad

Ingredients:
½ cup walnut halves
4-6 cups arugula, cleaned and dried
1 pear
Juice of 1 lemon
3 tablespoons extra-virgin olive oil,
   eyeball it
Himalayan sea salt, to taste
Freshly ground black pepper, to taste

Directions:
1. Toast nuts in small pan over medium heat until lightly toasted. Let cool.
2. Combine arugula and pear in a salad bowl, add nuts.
3. Add lemon juice, olive oil, salt, and pepper.
4. Toss and enjoy!

BLISS TIP

Slow down when eating and chew your food thoroughly to help your body absorb essential nutrients. You'll also get full sooner and won't overeat.

FALL BLISS DINNER

Roasted Brussels Sprouts and Brown Rice

Ingredients:
2 cups Brussels sprouts
½ cup brown rice, cooked
2 tbsp. olive oil
Sea salt and pepper, to taste

Directions:
1. Preheat oven to 425 °F.
2. Prepare rice as directed.
3. Cut Brussels sprouts in half and lay on baking sheet.
4. Brush olive oil over Brussels sprouts and sprinkle salt and pepper.
5. Bake 12-15 minutes or until golden brown.
6. Serve with rice and enjoy!

Sweet Potato Quesadilla

Ingredients:
1 small sweet potato
1 tbsp. cinnamon
1 gluten-free tortilla soft shell
¼ cup cooked black beans
¼ cup fresh pineapple, cubed
¼ cup almond "cheese" *(optional)**
1 tbsp. olive oil
Sea salt to taste

Directions:
1. Preheat oven to 400 °F.
2. Cut sweet potato into chunks and place on baking sheet. Lightly oil and add salt and cinnamon. Mix evenly. Bake until tender—approximately 15 minutes.
3. In small skillet, combine black beans and pineapple. Heat about 5 minutes.
4. In large skillet, gently heat tortilla on low heat.
5. Add black beans, sweet potato, pineapple and "cheese." Cook on medium heat until "cheese" is melted and tortilla shell is golden brown.
5. Enjoy!

Note: Almond cheese may be found in the health section of your supermarket or health food store.

Veggie Burger

Ingredients:

2 tbsp. olive oil

½ cup chopped onion

1 clove garlic, minced

1 cups diced veggies (suggestions: carrots, celery, mushrooms, chopped spinach, chopped kale, corn, chopped artichokes, zucchini, squash, sweet potato)

1 can of black beans, drained

1 tbsp. sesame oil

Spices, to taste (try cumin, cayenne, tumeric, and/or black pepper)

½ tsp. sea salt (omit or reduce if your liquid or spices contain salt)

½ cup quick oats

¼ cup leftover rice or quinoa

¼ cup milled flaxseed

Water (as necessary)

Directions:

1. Heat 2 teaspoons olive oil in a pan over medium heat. Fry the onion, garlic and veggies until softened, about 5 minutes. Let cool.

2. Transfer to a food processor and pulse with beans, sesame oil, spices, and salt until combined, but still chunky. Pulse in the oats, rice or quinoa, and flaxseed. (Note: You may need to add a little water as necessary.)

3. Make patties and heat over lightly oiled skillet. Fry patties 2-3 minutes per side or until golden brown.

4. Enjoy on a gluten-free bun with veggie toppings!

BLISS TIP

A balanced body starts with what you put on your plate. A good rule of thumb is to make sure half of your plate has vegetables on it, ¼ whole grain, and ¼ lean protein.

FALL BLISS DINNER

Quinoa with Roasted Root Vegetables

Ingredients:

3 tbsp. olive oil

2 medium sweet potatoes, peeled and
   cut into ½-inch cubes

5 parsnips, peeled and cut into
   4-inch cubes

6 shallots, peeled and cut into quarters

1 tbsp. rosemary

3 cloves garlic, minced

1 ½ cups vegetable broth or water

¾ cup quinoa, cooked

½ tsp. sea salt

½ tsp. black pepper

½ tsp. cumin

¼ tsp. cinnamon

Flat parsley for garnish

Optional toppings:

¼ cup chopped pecans

½ cup dried cranberries

Directions:

1. Preheat oven to 400 °F.

2. Coat baking pan with 1 tbsp. olive oil.

3. Place sweet potatoes, parsnips and
   shallots in bowl and toss with 1 tbsp.
   olive oil and rosemary.

4. Place veggies evenly on baking pan
   and bake for 45-55 minutes until soft,
   checking occasionally.

5. In large saucepan, heat 1 tbsp. olive oil
   on medium heat. Add garlic and sauté
   until garlic starts to brown.

6. Rinse quinoa thoroughly in cold water
   and drain in mesh strainer.

7. Add vegetable broth, quinoa, salt,
   pepper, cumin, and cinnamon to
   garlic and oil mixture. Bring to a boil,
   then reduce heat to medium-low,
   cover and simmer for 15-20 minutes.
   Set aside.

8. Once veggies are done baking, place
   quinoa in a bowl, stir in roasted
   veggies.

9. Garnish with parsley and toppings.
   Serve and enjoy!

Protein Power Spiced Quinoa

Ingredients:

1 tbsp. olive oil

1 small onion, chopped

3 cloves garlic, minced

¾ cup quinoa, dry

½ tsp. sea salt

½ tsp. black pepper

½ tsp. cumin

¼ tsp. cinnamon

1 ½ cups vegetable broth

One 15-oz. can chickpeas, drained and
   rinsed (Eden brand with BPA-free can
   lining is best)

½ cup walnuts, chopped

½ cup raisins or cranberries

½ cup chopped Italian/flat parsley

¾ cup roasted and cubed sweet
   potatoes (optional)

Directions:

1. In large saucepan, heat olive oil on medium heat. Add garlic and onion and sauté for 5 minutes.

2. Rinse quinoa thoroughly in cold water and drain in mesh strainer. Add quinoa, salt, pepper, cumin, cinnamon and vegetable broth to onion garlic mixture.

3. Bring to a boil, then reduce heat to medium-low, cover and simmer for 15-20 minutes.

4. Once quinoa has finished cooking, stir in chickpeas, walnuts, raisins or cranberries, and sweet potatoes.

5. Garnish with parsley, serve and enjoy!

BLISS TIP

Drink filtered water as much as possible throughout the day and at least eight 8-oz. glasses. Listen to your body and if you experience headaches or fatigue, these can be signs that you need more water. For extra hydration, try unsweetened coconut water.

FALL BLISS DINNER

Spaghetti Squash with Parsley and Cinnamon

Ingredients:
1 small spaghetti squash
1-½ tbsp. olive oil
2 cups chopped Italian/flat parsley
1 tsp. cinnamon
½ tsp. sea salt
¼ tsp. black pepper

Topping suggestions:
¼ cup walnuts, chopped
½ cup raisins

Directions:
1. Preheat oven to 375 °F.
2. Slice squash in half lengthwise. Using a large spoon, scoop out seeds and discard.
3. Coat large baking pan with olive oil.
4. Place each half of squash down on pan with skin side facing up. Bake for 45 minutes. Flip to other side and bake an additional 15 minutes.
5. Remove from oven and let cool for 5 minutes.
6. Using a fork, scrape out strings of squash and place in large bowl.
7. Toss with remaining ingredients and add optional toppings. Enjoy!

Veggie Bake

Ingredients:
Any leftover veggies that need to be used
1 large can chopped tomatoes
One 15-oz. can chickpeas
2-3 tbsp. olive oil

Directions:
1. Preheat oven to 400 °F.
2. Chop veggies and stir-fry in olive oil until soft.
3. Add can of tomatoes and drained can of chickpeas.
3. Place mixture in a casserole dish and bake 40 minutes or until top layer is golden brown.
5. Enjoy!

Drink peppermint, chamomile, ginger or other herbal teas with large meals or directly after. The warmth aids digestion. Organic nettle tea helps cleanse the blood and support your liver and kidneys.

keep it warm

For additional snack, drink and dessert recipes for all seasons, see pages 255-265!

FALL BLISS SHOPPING LIST

Vegetables

Spinach
Kale
Carrots
Cucumbers
Pumpkin
Onion
Assorted peppers: green, yellow, and red
Garlic
Celery
Bok choy
Collards
Mushrooms
Brussels sprouts
Sweet potatoes
Parsnips
Shallots
Spaghetti squash
Sugar snap peas

Fruits

Lemons
Bananas
Pineapple
Bing cherries
Assorted apples
Pears

Herbs

Parsley

Grains

Oatmeal
Rolled oats
Whole wheat, almond, or quinoa flour
Wild rice
Brown rice
Quinoa

Other

Almond, rice or coconut milk
Canned pumpkin
Carob chips
Cage-free organic eggs
Pecans
Vegetable broth
Gluten-free tortilla
Walnuts
Black beans
Raisins
Chickpeas
Dried cranberries
Pumpkin seeds
Popcorn
Almonds

BLISS TIP

For your convenience, this list is available to download and print at **www.BlissCleanse.com/fallshoplist**

The Daily Bliss Checklist is a wonderful tool to help you stay on track each day of the two-week program. For your convenience, this list is available to download and print at www.BlissCleanse.com/checklist

focus

DAILY **BLISS CHECKLIST**

Today's Date:_____

❑ Start my day with a positive thought such as: "Today is a great day!"

❑ Balance my body by drinking 16 oz filtered water with fresh squeezed juice of ½ lemon upon waking.

❑ Say my favorite affirmation(s) in front of the mirror in the morning. (Examples: "I love my body," "I am beautiful," "I live my bliss," "I am healthy, vibrant, and whole.")

❑ Reflect on 3-5 things I am grateful for, jotting them down in my gratitude journal, and notice how I feel when I think about them, either at morning or night.

❑ Choose a self-care activity for today and a time I will do it:

    ❑ detox bath/time:_____   ❑ hot towel scrub /time: _____

    ❑ listen to the guided meditations/time:_____   other/time:_____

❑ My exercise plan for the day and time I will do this:

    ❑ walk or run/time:_____   ❑ workout at the gym/time:_____

    ❑ yoga/exercise class/time: _____   ❑ other/time: _____   ❑ rest day

❑ If I'm on the go today, then pack healthy snacks such as raw nuts and seeds, cut carrots and celery, and fresh or dried fruit, along with filtered water, so I'll have them on hand when hunger strikes.

❑ Drink at least 64 oz. of filtered water and herbal teas. Drink even more when I can to aid the cleansing process.

❑ Review Today's Daily Bliss Inspiration. Try out any recommended activities that inspire me.

❑ Eat a healthy and satisfying breakfast, review my *Bliss Cleanse* Guidelines if necessary. Follow my Seasonal Cleansing Guides with recipes and meal plans for ideas.

❑ Eat a healthy mid-morning snack.

❑ Eat a healthy and satisfying lunch. This should be my biggest meal of the day.

❑ Eat a healthy afternoon snack.

❑ Eat a light, clean, yet satisfying dinner. Cook enough for at least two meals. My dinner should be 50% or more greens.

❑ One thing I appreciate about myself today: _____

❑ One thing I am looking forward to tomorrow: _____

❑ End my day with a positive thought such as, "I had a wonderful day and now I will have a wonderful rest."

❑ Get at least 8-9 hours of sleep.

get inspired

YOUR FALL BLISS
DAILY INSPIRATIONS

We are so excited to bring you our daily inspirations, the ***prized gem of this program!*** Be sure to allow time each day to read and experience these most powerful tips.

If you feel the tendency to say, "I'll do it later," then commit now to giving yourself permission to complete each day's exercise on the day it was intended, rather than put it off, in order to fully embrace the purpose and intention of your mind-body-spirit *Bliss Cleanse*. You are worth it!!!

By following these tips each day, you will nourish yourself with the self-care needed to truly benefit from this program. Remember it's not about doing every-thing, it's about doing a few things each day to support you on your path to bliss.

What's great about these inspirations is that you have them to use after the cleanse is over!

Celebrate your success on taking this journey. You owe it to yourself!

Love,

Lindsey & Lorraine

DAY **ONE**

Since today is the first day of the Fall *Bliss Cleanse,* we want you to set your intentions *in writing.* Your chances of succeeding with this or any program are greatly increased when you set an intention. This helps you get clear on what you want to achieve.

So grab a journal or notebook or use the space below and let's get started!

What are you hoping to achieve from this program?

What will be the benefit to you once you have achieved it (your "WHY")?

What are ready to let go of? Perhaps you are ready to let go of a physical condition such as excess weight, tension, chronic headaches, skin problems, fatigue, or brittle hair and nails. Think about which things you are most ready to let go of. Next think about what mental or emotional conditions you want to release such as anxiety, emotional ups and downs, negativity, anger, frustration, or fear. *Write them down.*

What are you ready to bring in? Now write down a few things you are ready to bring into your life, to replace what you will be letting go. How do you want to feel come winter?

When you're finished, take a moment to thank yourself for completing today's activity!

DAY TWO

Today is all about gratitude!

Simply write down 3-5 things you are grateful for, and focus on how you feel when you think about them. We recommend getting a separate journal or notebook to do this, and practicing gratitude either first thing in the morning, or last thing before going to bed. *From Gratitude to Bliss*® is an excellent tool to help you begin your practice. Plan to practice gratitude every day during this cleanse and beyond.

When you're finished, take a moment to thank yourself for completing today's activity!

DAY **THREE**

We live in such a fast-paced society, that we often forget to slow down and appreciate the moment. We not only forget to slow down and appreciate the moment, but we forget to slow down and appreciate our food.

For today, really appreciate your food for nourishing you and taking care of your body. Take time to slow down and appreciate each bite and chew. Really notice the taste, smell, color, and texture of the food before you. Think about how eating fall foods such as root vegetables and squashes helps you stay in tune with the season. Put your fork down after every bite. Breathe, be silent, and give thanks.

Write down any differences you notice. Is this something you can work on incorporating on a daily basis?

When you're finished, take a moment to thank yourself for completing today's activity!

DAY **FOUR**

"What we think about ourselves becomes the
truth for us ... Every thought we think is creating our
future. Each one of us creates our experiences by our
thoughts and our feelings. The thoughts we think and
the words we speak create our experiences."

–Louise Hay, *You Can Heal Your Life*[1]

**How are you talking to yourself today? Are you lifting yourself up or are
you tearing yourself down?**

Pay extra attention to how you are talking to yourself. Notice when you say
something negative and try to replace it with something positive instead.

For example, if you find yourself saying, "It's just so hard for me to lose weight."
Instead say," I love my body and it's easy to lose weight."

It may sound silly at first, but over time, you will start thinking better and
feeling better!

When you're finished, take a moment to thank yourself for completing today's activity!

[1] Hay, Louise. You Can Heal Your Life. New York: Hay House, 1984.

DAY **FIVE**

Are you being present in day-to-day situations?

Start by simply being present in your own life. Find peace and joy in nature and your surroundings. Smile at someone walking down the hall or the sidewalk. Simply put, just be.

Appreciate the current moment for what it is, right now. Make it a discipline to stop and appreciate each moment in your life.

Challenge yourself with this exercise:

Take a mindful walk and ...

- Walk slowly.
- Stop.
- Look at the intricate details in your surroundings. What changes have you noticed now that it's fall?
- See the veins on leaves, the insects crawling on trees, and the different colors in front of you.
- Now hear the birds chirping, the wind blowing in the background, or the crinkle of leaves beneath animal feet.
- Stop once again. Would you have noticed these things if you had not made the effort to be present?

When you're finished, take a moment to thank yourself for completing today's activity!

DAY **SIX**

You're almost halfway through the mind-body-spirit *Bliss Cleanse* and you are doing an amazing job! When you give your body time to rest and replenish, you start feeling so much better!

Because we are all bio-individually different, however, we all respond to cleansing differently at first.

Pay attention to how are you feeling this week—emotionally and physically. Are you more energetic and happy? Or are you more lethargic and moody?

Pay attention to how your body is feeling and reacting. Journal your thoughts!

When you're finished, take a moment to thank yourself for completing today's activity!

DAY **SEVEN**

It's one thing to eat healthy and cleanse yourself physically, but it is also just as important to cleanse yourself emotionally.

Often times, we let past wounds take foot in our lives and shape us into someone we are not. So instead of dwelling, we want you to list all the reasons why you are amazing! Shifting from a negative to a positive light can not only spread happiness, but it can also shed "weight" we have been carrying around for years.

Why are YOU amazing? What qualities make you amazing, inside and out?

Embrace those qualities by recording them below. When you aren't feeling so good about yourself, look back on your list and remember all your beautiful qualities.

I am amazing because:

When you're finished, take a moment to thank yourself for completing today's activity!

DAY **EIGHT**

You're halfway there! WOOO-HOOO! Way to go! Stop and appreciate this success and the other successes along the way.

We are always trying to get to an end result, and we often dismiss the small successes along the way. Stop and appreciate the successes you had just this morning: making yourself a delish breakfast, taking the kids to school, or sending out a birthday card.

You have accomplished a week-long cleanse! That is a huge success in itself! What other successes have you noticed this week? Take a moment to reflect on all the good that has happened this past week. Write them down!

My recent successes:

When you're finished, take a moment to thank yourself for completing today's activity!

DAY **NINE**

Take some time and focus on stretching today – whether it is in the morning, at your work desk, at a meeting, etc.

Take some time to do some simple stretches to get your blood flowing!

Stretching not only increases your flexibility and helps relieve pain, but it can also generate better blood circulation which helps brings nutrients to your cells AND flushes out toxins. So really, it's a win-win!

Get stretching!

When you're finished, take a moment to thank yourself for completing today's activity!

DAY **TEN**

It's no secret that regular exercise is good for you. It's not only important to try light exercises that help you stretch and strengthen, but it's also important to try exercises that help you break a sweat! Sweating helps release the built up toxins from the winter months and also helps tighten your skin!

Not there yet? Listen to your body and take it slow. If you're feeling a little tired, get outside and walk! A 10-minute walk is enough to increase energy and improve mood for up to two hours!

When you're finished, take a moment to thank yourself for completing today's activity!

DAY **ELEVEN**

Focus on spreading your love and light into the world by paying it forward. Focus today on doing small things for others. These small things could make a huge difference in someone's life!

Here are some suggestions to get you started, but remember to use your creativity and make this practice authentic to you! Use the space at the end to add your own ideas. Try something new with each season.

- Buy a stranger coffee when you find yourself waiting in line
- Put a quarter in a meter that is about to expire
- Smile at a stranger
- Tip a server generously
- Donate to your favorite charity
- Compliment someone in the checkout line
- Volunteer at a local shelter
- Hold the door for someone
- Offer advice to a friend
- Invite someone to cut in front of you at the grocery store
- Donate blood
- _____
- _____
- _____
- _____
- _____

When you're finished, take a moment to thank yourself for completing today's activity!

DAY **TWELVE**

Take some time out today to focus on meditation. Meditation is a way to let go of outside stressors and key in on what's really important!

Practice Easy Meditation: Take a 5-15 minute break every day, close your eyes and focus on your breath. Breathe in something you are grateful for. Breathe out any stress you may be feeling in your body. If your mind wanders, simply bring it back to your breath.

Also check out the *Bliss Meditation Collection* for a guided approach to getting started, available at **www.BlissCleanse.com/shop.**

When you're finished, take a moment to thank yourself for completing today's activity!

DAY **THIRTEEN**

Cleansing in all areas is really important. We have been working on the body and the mind, but today let's look at your space!

Out with the old; in with the new! "Spring" cleaning can be the most cleansing act of them all and can be done with each season! Whether it's sorting through and clearing out old clothes, organizing your closets and kitchen cabinets, or finishing incomplete projects, cleaning up is a refreshing and feel-good process. Hello, peace of mind!

Start small with one space or room and work your way up! You will be complete before you know it! And remember—it's not a race!

If this seems too overwhelming, simply aim to de-clutter at least one area of your home—a room, a closet, or your files—with each season.

When you're finished, take a moment to thank yourself for completing today's activity!

DAY **FOURTEEN**

Congratulations!

Today is the last day of your *Bliss Fall Cleanse!* Stop and savor your success in taking this amazing journey to your health and happiness. Reflect on the areas you want to continue with and set your intentions moving forward.

Honor those intentions. Move forward blissfully. And remember that small changes lead to big results!

Woo-hoo!
Way to go!!!

take note

BLISS TIP

Use the pages that follow to make notes during the Fall *Bliss Cleanse.* These will prove helpful when you return this winter!

TODAY'S DATE:

· ·

What I found helpful...

What I found challenging...

TODAY'S DATE:

. . . .

What I want to work on next time...

Recipes I want to try next time...

TODAY'S DATE:

....

TODAY'S DATE:

TODAY'S DATE:

....

TODAY'S DATE:

. . . .

TODAY'S DATE:

. . . .

TODAY'S DATE:

TODAY'S DATE:

TODAY'S DATE:

satisfy

BLISS
SNACKS
DRINKS &
DESSERTS
FOR ALL SEASONS

BLISS SNACKS

Original Hummus

Ingredients:
2 cups canned chickpeas
1-3 cloves garlic
3 tbsp. tahini
½ tsp. sea salt
2 tbsp. olive oil (optional)
2 tbsp. lemon juice
½ cup or more spring water, use chickpea water

Directions:
1. Place all ingredients in a blender and purée until creamy.
2. Add more garlic, tahini, or lemon juice to taste.
3. Serve with pita bread, fresh veggies, or crackers.

Cucumber Sliders

Ingredients:
1-2 large cucumbers
Hummus

Directions:
1. Cut cucumber in ½-inch round slices.
2. Add hummus to a slice and close off with another slice on top, making a mini sandwich.
3. Serve and enjoy!

BLISS TIP

Keep a food journal. Examine where and when you experience cravings, important clues to determining what your body may be needing to get back into balance.

Mini Veggie Muffins

Ingredients:

1 cup veggies, grated or finely chopped
(suggestions: carrots, zucchini, squash,
peppers, onions)

2 eggs, beaten

2 cups spelt flour

½ cup parsley, finely chopped

1 cup soy or rice milk

Pinch of sea salt

Directions:

1. Preheat oven to 325 degrees.
2. Mix flour and salt in a bowl.
3. Make a well, add eggs, veggies and parsley.
4. Mix lightly, gradually add milk. This is supposed to be lumpy so don't work too hard!
5. Spoon into a mini muffin tray that is lightly oiled.
6. Bake for 12-15 minutes.
7. Remove and allow to set for 10 minutes, then serve.

Kale Chips

Ingredients:

1 to 2 bunches kale

Olive oil

Nutritional yeast

Himalayan Sea Salt

Directions:

1. Preheat oven to 425 degrees F.
2. Remove kale from stalk, leaving the greens in large pieces.
3. Place a little olive oil in a bowl, dip your fingers and rub a very light coat of oil over the kale.
4. Place kale on baking sheet and sprinkle nutritional yeast and Himalayan sea salt to taste.
5. Bake for 5 minutes or until it starts to turn a bit brown. Turn the kale over and bake with the other side up. Keep an eye on it as it can burn quickly.
6. Remove and serve.

BLISS SNACKS

Sweet Potato Chips

Ingredients:
1 to 2 sweet potatoes
Olive oil
Himalayan sea salt

Directions:
1. Preheat oven to 425 degrees F.
2. Remove skin from sweet potatoes.
3. Cut sweet potatoes in thin, chip like slices and remove any extra moisture.
4. Place a little olive oil in a bowl, dip your fingers and rub a very light coat of oil over the sweet potatoes.
5. Place on baking sheet and sprinkle Himalayan sea salt to taste.
6. Bake for 10 minutes and flip to the other side.
7. Bake another 5-10 minutes until golden brown.
8. Remove, cool, and serve.

BLISS TIP

Always balance carbs and protein, especially if you have a blood sugar issue. For example, eat an apple with almond butter, raisins with nuts, or carrots and hummus.

Quick & Easy Granola Bars

Ingredients:
3 cups quick oats
3 tbsp. chia seeds
½ cup unsalted peanuts, chopped
½ cup extra dark or vegan
   chocolate chips
¾ cup peanut butter, melted
½ cup brown rice syrup

Directions:
1. In a large bowl, combine oats, chia seeds, peanuts, and chocolate chips.
2. Slowly add in the peanut butter and brown rice syrup.
3. Mix until the mixture forms one large ball.
4. Press dough into a 4 x 13 baking dish.
5. Refrigerate up to 60 minutes.
6. Cut into squares and enjoy!

Easy Energy Bars

Ingredients:
½ cup raw cashews, chopped
½ cup raw almonds, chopped
½ cup raw peanuts, chopped
½ cup sunflower seeds, chopped
1 ½ cup quick oats
½ cup almond or peanut butter, melted
1/3 cup brown rice syrup or
   honey, melted

Directions:
1. In a large bowl, combine cashews, almonds, peanuts, and sunflower seeds.
2. Slowly add in almond or peanut butter and honey or brown rice syrup.
3. Mix until the mixture turns into one solid ball.
4. Take the mixture and press into a lined 8 x 8 pan.
5. Refrigerate for 60 minutes, cut into squares, and enjoy!

BLISS DRINKS

Tea Latte

Ingredients:
Your favorite tea
¼ - ½ cup almond, soy, or
  coconut milk
Honey, to sweeten

Directions:
1. Steep your favorite hot tea.
2. In saucepan, heat your favorite milk
   and whisk for about 5-10 minutes.
   Add honey to sweeten, if necessary.
3. Add milk to steeped tea, stir,
   and enjoy!

Tummy Calming Tea

Ingredients:
4 thick slices of fresh ginger
2 slices of lemon
1 ½ cups water

Directions:
1. Boil water in small saucepan.
2. When it comes to a boil, add fresh
   ginger and lower heat.
3. Steep about 3-5 minutes.
4. Pour into a mug and add lemons.
5. Enjoy!

Nutty Hot Chocolate

Ingredients:
1 tbsp. raw cacao
1 cup unsweetened almond milk
1-2 tsp. honey

Directions:
1. In a small saucepan, combine
   almond milk and raw cacao and
   bring to small boil.
2. Reduce heat and use a whisk to turn
   almond milk a chocolate color.
3. Keep whisking and add in honey
   to sweeten.
4. Remove from heat, pour into mug,
   and enjoy!

Bliss Water

Ingredients:
Water
Your favorite fruit, herbs, and spices (such as lemon, lime, orange, strawberry, ginger, mint, lemongrass, lavendar, or vanilla)

Directions:
1. Slice and add your favorite fruit, herbs, or spices to a pitcher of water.
2. Chill one-hour before serving.
3. Add ice and enjoy

Variations:
Citrus blend of oranges, lemons, and limes
Limeade blend with limes, lemons, and raspberries
Fresh watermelon and mint
Fresh strawberries and basil
Lemongrass, with mint and vanilla

BLISS TIP

Use only natural sweeteners. Raw honey, pure maple syrup, organic agave, or stevia. Avoid all foods including breads and sauces that contain refined sugar. *Optional: you may choose to avoid all sugars during this cleanse, including natural sweeteners, to see how your body reacts to being free of sugar.*

BLISS DESSERTS

Chocolate Chip Quinoa Cookies

Ingredients:
2 cups cooked quinoa (typically about
   1-1 ½ cup dry)
¾ cup quick or rolled oats
½ tsp. sea salt
1 tbsp. cinnamon
2 tbsp. maple syrup
½ cup almond butter
½ cup dark chocolate chips

Directions:
1. Preheat oven to 350 degrees F.
2. Cook quinoa as directed and let cool.
3. In a separate bowl, combine oats, sea salt, and cinnamon.
4. Once quinoa is cool, add maple syrup, almond butter, and finally, chocolate chips. Mix well.
5. Scoop into 1 inch round balls on non-stick cookie tray. Cook for 20 minutes or until bottom of the cookie is brown.
6. Let cool and enjoy!

Chunky Monkey Ice Cream

Ingredients:
Peeled and cut frozen banana pieces
   (equivalent to 1 banana)
¼ cup unsweetened almond or
   coconut milk
1 tbsp. organic peanut or almond butter
1 tbsp. dark chocolate chips

Directions:
1. Combine frozen bananas, milk, and nut butter in small blender. Blend until soft like soft serve ice cream.
2. Pour in dish and sprinkle dark chocolate chips on top.
3. Enjoy!

Chunky Monkey Banana Bites

Ingredients:
1 banana
Nut butter
Dark chocolate chips

Directions:
1. Slice banana into ½ inch coins.
2. Place one coin down and add a small scoop of nut butter on top.
3. Sprinkle a few chocolate chips on top.
4. Place a banana coin slice on top of the nut butter and chocolate chips. It will look like a little mini sandwich.
5. Enjoy!

Simple Raspberry Bites

Ingredients:
6 raspberries
6 dark vegan chocolate chips

Directions:
1. Wash raspberries and dry.
2. Place chocolate chip in the opening of the raspberry.
3. Enjoy this quick and easy treat!

Chocolatey Chia Pudding

Ingredients:
1 cup unsweetened almond or coconut milk
2 tbsp. raw cacao powder
¼ cup chia seeds
¼ cup maple syrup

Directions:
1. Combine milk and raw cacao powder in a small mixing bowl and mix until the cacao powder is blended in.
2. Add chia seeds and maple syrup and mix well.
3. Let chill/set in the fridge for 2-3 hours.
4. Enjoy!

BLISS DESSERTS

Crunchy Bliss Bites

Ingredients:
½ cup cashews

¼ cup coconut shreds

¾ cup quick oats

1 tsp. sea salt

2 tbsp. raw cacao

6 tsp. coconut oil

2 tsp. raw honey

½ cup almond butter

Directions:
1. Process cashews and coconut shreds in food processor until fine. For a little crunch, process a little less.
2. Place mixture in a bowl and add oats, sea salt and raw cacao. Stir.
3. Add coconut oil and mix.
4. Gradually mix in honey and almond butter until the mixture becomes one ball.
5. Take mixture and roll into little balls. This mixture makes about 12.

BONUS TIP:
Freeze the bites for a late night sweet craving without the guilt!

Raw Chocolate Truffles

Ingredients:
½ cup coconut butter or oil
¾ cup agave nectar
¼ tsp. sea salt
2 tsp. vanilla extract
1 ¼ cup dried shredded coconut
2 ¼ cups raw cacao powder
¼ cup chopped pistachio nuts
¼ cup chopped walnuts

Directions:

1. Blend coconut oil, agave, sea salt and vanilla in a blender. If coconut oil is solid, place in double boiler to warm gently (do not heat directly).

2. Add 1 cup shredded coconut, ½ cup at a time and blend until smooth.

3. Transfer to bowl and add 2 cups of cacao powder. Mix evenly.

4. Refrigerate for 20 minutes allowing the mixture to set.

5. When mixture has thickened, roll heaping tablespoons into balls. (For smaller truffles, use heaping teaspoons).

6. Place remaining cacao, coconut, pistachios and walnuts on separate plates.

7. Roll each ball in one of the 4 toppings and refrigerate until ready to serve.
   Yields 40 small truffles. Enjoy!

Even healthy sweets should be eaten sparingly. We've provided these healthy dessert recipes to allow you to enjoy some sweetness without any guilt, but be careful not to over-indulge. Even natural sugar can be addicting and can weaken your immune system when eaten in excess.

continue

AFTER THE CLEANSE

Now that you have completed the mind-body-spirit *Bliss Cleanse* program, remember that everything you learned can stay with you throughout your life. Think about which areas of the program resonated with you most and commit to bringing one or two lifestyle choices with you even now that the cleanse is over.

Like many of our clients, you too may find that cleansing four times a year, at the start of each season, brings a sense of renewal and reinforcement to your health and happiness goals. Seasonal cleansing not only feels good, it also helps you to continually own particular lifestyle choices as part of your everyday routine, while gradually bringing in a few more changes throughout the year.

Connect with us!
We love hearing how our cleansers are doing with this program. Feel free to drop us a line at: **FindYourBliss@BlissCleanse.com** and share your experience and success with us!

Need extra support?
Should you find you need extra support to continue following the guidelines and tools presented in this cleanse, please reach out to us to learn about our individual and group coaching programs. We will work with you to find the program that best suits your needs and help you stay focused on your journey to vibrant health and lasting happiness!

For more information about our coaching services, programs and tools please visit: **www.BlissCleanse.com!**

Wishing you a life of bliss!

Lindsey & Lorraine

about

LINDSEY SMITH
Motivational Speaker, Holistic Health Coach, and Author

Lindsey Smith began her cycle of binge eating at age four. Her foods of choice were Swedish Goldfish, Watermelon Sour Patch Gummies, and blue Flying Saucers. With a background like that, you can count on Lindsey to demonstrate compassion and humor as well as powerful insights into your relationship with food.

After overcoming childhood anxiety and weight gain through discovering the connection between foods and moods, Lindsey immersed herself in studying the emotional connections people have with food. She learned that when people look to food for nutrients like acceptance, comfort, celebration, and love, a disastrous cycle of junk foods and junk moods begins. This insight, combined with Lindsey's expertise as a certified Health Coach, means Lindsey is ideally qualified to help clients gain freedom over destructive food habits.

Founder of "The Real You," Lindsey serves clients as a keynote speaker, a one-on-one coach, and author of the book, *Junk Foods and Junk Moods.*

She helps clients lose weight, increase energy, and gain a healthy lifestyle by uncovering their personal connection with the foods they eat and their moods.

Lindsey's approach is not a quick-fix, quick-fail diet, but rather a journey toward understanding yourself and the food choices you make. Her solutions are not designed to make clients sacrifice or deprive themselves for health, but to make small changes that build to big results.

Lindsey shares a personal story that shows she's been there and overcame obstacles at a young age. Her positive attitude and humor has been a crowd pleaser to many audiences, including the Pennsylvania Nutrition Education Network, WIC Family Services, the Pennsylvania Mental Health Consumer Association, and PNC Bank.

Whether you work with Lindsey one-on-one, engage her to deliver a presentation, or read *Junk Foods and Junk Moods,* you can be sure you will laugh, cry, and find inspiring solutions to your own problems with food and mood relationships!

LORRAINE MILLER
Holistic Lifestyle Coach, Inspirational Speaker and Author

Lorraine Miller, HC, AADP is a Holistic Lifestyle Coach and author of the award-winning journal, *From Gratitude to Bliss®: A Journey in Health and Happiness*. Having recognized the amazing transformational power a regular gratitude practice has had in her own life, Lorraine is focused on sharing the power of gratitude with everyone she meets. For nearly eight years, Lorraine was on a quest to become a Mom, a challenging journey of ups and downs which at times has caused her chronic stress, fatigue, depression, and despair. But in early 2010, Lorraine began keeping a gratitude journal, a tool she says was, "a true gift that allowed me to turn everything around in my life. I kept hoping for a tool to help me with my struggle. I didn't want to live in emotional pain any more." Lucky for her, the universe showed up and gave her a tool that continues to provide her with peace, joy and at times, Lorraine says, "moments of bliss."

From coaching clients and teaching workshops, to creating inspirational tools and programs, Lorraine shares her inspiring message which provides a key ingredient to opening one's mind and heart to receiving all the good in the world. Through this process she says, "We begin to heal, to move, and to choose our own destiny."

Lorraine believes in looking to nature first as a way to nourish all areas of life. Her company, Nourish By Nature, Inc. serves to inspire vibrant health and lasting happiness.

Whether you need support through a difficult life challenge, or simply want to find more joy and greater health, Lorraine's simple yet holistic approach allows you to connect to your true self and move in the direction that serves you best.

Lorraine holds a BS in Business and Economics from Lehigh University, a BFA in Graphic Design from the School of Visual Arts, a Certificate in Acupressure and Shiatsu from the Acupressure Institute, a Certificate in Foot Reflexology from the New York Open Center, and a Certificate in Health Coaching from the Institute for Integrative Nutrition, and is certified by the Association for Drugless Practitioners.

Lorraine lives with her husband, Daniel, on the north shore of Long Island, just outside of New York City. They are expecting their first child in Spring 2013!

Connect with Lorraine at **NourishByNature.com** and Discover What Feeds You!™

connect

CLEANSE WITH US **LIVE!**

Each season, we offer a LIVE Virtual *Bliss Cleanse* Program to give you additional support and tools to enhance your cleansing experience.

In this live two-week course, you will not only gain everything in the *Bliss Cleanse,* you will also receive additional tools and community support.

The two-week experience includes:

- 2 LIVE group coaching calls
- A bonus "Ask The Coach" call—where you can dial in and get your questions answered
- Access to a community support group with fellow cleansers
- Instructional videos including recipes, self-care, pantry must-haves, and more
- Bonus Recipes not included in the book
- Daily Inspirational emails to keep you on track
- Bonus Bliss Meditations

To cleanse with us LIVE, visit **www.BlissCleanse.com** to register!

2045783R00150

Made in the USA
San Bernardino, CA
05 March 2013